Postcards
from the Edge of
FOOTBALL
A Social History of a British Game
HUNTER DAVIES

MAINSTREAM
PUBLISHING
EDINBURGH AND LONDON

Copyright © Hunter Davies, 2010

First published in Great Britain in 2010 by
MAINSTREAM PUBLISHING COMPANY (EDINBURGH) LTD
7 Albany Street
Edinburgh EH1 3UG

ISBN 9781845965587

A catalogue record for this book is available from the British Library

Text design by Gill McColl

Typeset in Caslon, Futura and Marcelle Script

Printed in Great Britain by
Butler Tanner & Dennis Ltd, Frome, Somerset

ACKNOWLEDGEMENTS

The illustrations in this book are postcards from my own collection. With the captions in the book which accompany each postcard, I have mainly tried to describe the contents, interest or importance and estimate the date. The list of illustrations at the end of this book is an attempt, where possible, to identify the artists, photographers and postcard publishers, though alas a great many of the cards contain no clues, on either side, to their creators. The point of listing credits is to give credit, acknowledge those who produced those cards, so thank you very much indeed, but it is also to help those who might be so totally fascinated by a certain card that they want to track down a copy for themselves and need a few facts to go on. If a card is not listed it means the back is blank, there is no clue to its origin or creator, or at least none that I can decipher. Whenever possible I have tried to date and credit them, but I apologise to all those long-gone photographers and designers and artists I have not been able to identify but whose work I have used. With more modern cards, I have tried my best to contact the publishers and give due credit to the creators, but again this has not always been possible. I will make amends in future editions if I have missed any necessary credits. I am particularly grateful to the Football Association for permission to reproduce cards that they own, also to the National Portrait Gallery, the National Football Museum, Stuart Clarke, Mark Richards, Boomerang, Rev. Roger Lee, Lorenzo Agius and Nick Bull of Getty Images. Scans of certain cards, giving me better images than the ones I have, were kindly provided by Phil Smith of Bloomsbury Collector's Fair and Graham Budd of Graham Budd Associates and Sotheby's.

Also, personal thanks for help to Eric Krieger, David Barber of the FA and Kevin Moore and Peter Holme of the National Football Museum.

Contents

INTRODUCTION

Football is the world's most popular game. It's the beautiful game, it's the people's game, it's a funny old game, all things we tell ourselves, we trillions of football fans all over the world.

I like to think when I am going to a game, anywhere, that I am communing with millions of other fans doing exactly the same thing, all over the world, watching the same game, with the same rules, using very much the same language – as the words for 'goal' and 'penalty' and 'football' have been adopted by most languages. I like to imagine I am experiencing much the same emotions, effing and blinding along with trillions of others, in, of course, our own words and accents.

I also like to think I am communing with football fans in the past, that I am part of that vast global brotherhood – and sisterhood – who have gone before, who have played the game, watched the game, loved the game. It is true in one sense, as Bill Shankly said, that football is more important than life and death, in that it goes on, and will go on, long after our lives and our deaths. At least I hope it will. Be a poor do otherwise.

I've been thinking of football's past for well over 40 years, since I was at the 1966 World Cup final and deliberately kept every scrap, including my ticket and the nasty World Cup Willie postcards and mementos, telling myself 'this is an historic moment, it will probably not happen again in my lifetime, certainly not England winning a final'.

I began to wonder about past historic moments, how football started, who were the stars in the early days, the great teams, the great events, where did nets come from or were they always there?

Since then I have collected a great deal of football memorabilia, which was pretty cheap 40 years ago, then the prices started to soar once Sotheby's and Christie's came on the football scene. Investors arrived, some with very little real interest in the game, hoping prices would go up and up, but fortunately such investors seem mainly to have disappeared. Collectors of football memorabilia do tend to be real football fans.

I don't collect shirts, especially the allegedly autographed shirts, as I always suspect fiddles. Anyway, what can you do with a shirt? Do you

"SORRY REF., BUT SOMEONE'S BEEN MESSING ABOUT WITH MY LOCKER."

Comic footer cards will be coming later, please contain yourselves, but here is a taster of the highly amusing cards which were very popular at seasides in the 1950s.

hang it up, frame it, wear it, shove it in a drawer? I much prefer stuff that has content, which I can read and study, stare at and enjoy. So in my collection of 3,000 or so football items, it's mainly books, programmes, magazines and, most of all, postcards.

I started looking for ones of my favourite team, Tottenham Hotspur, and then any of the well-known professional teams, as long as the postcards and the teams depicted were old enough, say from somewhere between 1900 and 1939. They were relatively cheap, between about four and eight pounds, when I first began.

Alas, those days have gone. I don't know whether it has been investors who have put the prices up, or because football fans are better off, or if it's simply a matter of inflation. I prefer, though, to believe that it is because today there is a real interest in the history of football. People genuinely want to know more about how it all started. It could also be mingled with patriotism, wanting to enjoy and feel proud of Britain's contribution to the game.

So about ten years ago I mostly gave up looking for famous clubs, once I'd seen the prices, and found myself collecting postcards of un-famous clubs – those semi-professional, junior, district, local, amateur, school, college, factory, rural, ad hoc, knockabout teams.

You see them all the time at postcard fairs, at car boots, jumbles, often mixed up with other categories, other boxes. The players are unnamed, unremembered, long gone. The teams and clubs are mostly forgotten as well. Often only the initials live on. But I still buy them whenever and wherever I see them, regardless of the fact that I don't know anything at all about them.

I look into their innocent faces, wondering what became of them. I study their shirts, boots, shorts, trying to date them. I look for clues in the background. As my collection of Unknown Teams grew, I started to subdivide them, making up my own categories.

At the same time, I am always on the lookout for comic cards featuring football, the players

Above: One of the Great Unknown teams, circa 1910, which I can study for ages, looking in their faces, wondering what became of them, where did they buy those caps.

Right: One hundred years later, today's most well-known football event, the World Cup. Postcard for South Africa 2010.

or the language, or for advertising cards using a football image – for any sort of cards, really, that have a football element. Postcards, after all, are a visual record of our social history, and football postcards reflect the history of football.

It then struck me that the height of postcard mania, around 1900, was roughly coincidental with the height of football mania – the period when football first properly established itself as a dominant force in popular culture. So the histories of the two, postcards and football, are intertwined, each reflecting the other. I like to think I have therefore stumbled upon a new topic – the history of football as seen through postcards – which is getting a bit carried away, but that's what collectors do.

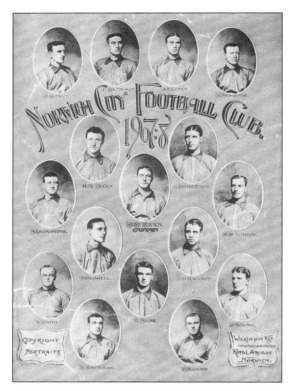

Classic team card, prettily arranged:
Norwich City, 1907–08.

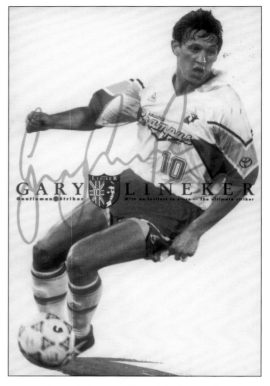

A real Known, Gary Lineker with
Grampus Eight, Japan, 1993.

Obviously, a full history of football can't possibly be told solely through postcards, but then again, loads of so called 'full' histories and encyclopaedias of football have already been produced, a lot of them filled with too many stats and league tables for my liking. And they have missed out postcards in going for the bigger picture (bigger in size but not always bigger in content, as postcards, as we shall see, reveal much that is hidden).

This history is therefore only a sideways look at football. By examining football postcards, how they mirrored and recorded and commented on what was going on in football and in mainstream life, I hope to illustrate, in both senses of the word, the importance of football and its place in the cultural and social history of the last 150 years. Right, let's kick off . . .

Chapter One

THE HISTORY OF POSTCARDS

What is a football postcard? My definition is a postcard that carries a football image, whether it's a player or a team, a piece of action or a piece of football equipment, anything really to do with football, and it can be photographic or artwork, serious or comic.

What is a postcard? Ah, that is harder to define and more complicated to explain. The first postcards were non-illustrated, that is they were simply pieces of card issued by the Post Office on which you could write a message. They first appeared in 1870. The Rev. Francis Kilvert, author of a famous diary, was one of the earliest to use them. On Tuesday, 4 October 1870, he wrote, 'Today I sent my first postcards, to my mother, Therise, Emma and Perch. They are capital things, simple, useful and handy. A happy invention.'

They came pre-stamped. You wrote the address on one side, where it had the halfpenny stamped and said POSTCARD, and the message on the other side. By law, no other sort of postcard was allowed at first.

The postcards were plain, with no fancy stuff, but in 1890 a rather elaborate prepaid envelope came out to celebrate the 50th anniversary of the Penny Post. (In 1840, Rowland Hill had introduced the penny black, the world's first prepaid postage stamp. Before that you paid when you collected your letter, from the postie or post office, and the price depended on the weight and how far it had come.) This 1890 envelope had inside it a postcard on which you could write on both sides, as it was going inside an envelope. I hope that's clear.

Illustrated postcards produced by independent manufacturers, as opposed to the official Post Office, started appearing in the UK around 1894 when the Post Office finally and belatedly relaxed its rules. They had been in use in Europe for some years, the first known illustrated postcards having appeared in Austria in 1869.

They came in odd shapes, some of them more square than what we term today 'postcard size', and you had to write the address on one side, and on the other, where the illustration was, you could write your message. This rather mucked

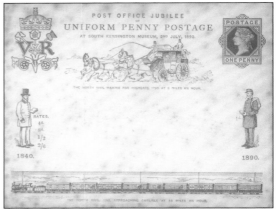

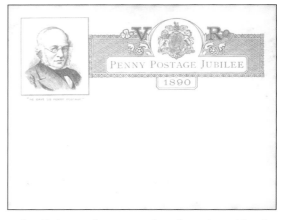

Above left: The UK's first postcards, 1870, were produced by the Post Office, pre—stamped but not illustrated. You wrote the address on one side, the message on the other.

Above right and right: In 1890, to celebrate 50 years of the Penny Post, a fancy decorated envelope had a card inside on which you could write a message.

up the illustration, whether photographic or artwork, as a space had to be left beside it for any message. Sometimes the space was titchy, other times you had space beside the illustration to write a few sentences, as in the postcard showing a goalkeeper saving the ball with the handwritten words beside saying, 'Just in time.' (What was clever was that although these three words were printed, they looked as if they had been written by hand – a device known in postcard circles as 'write-away' – which you continued with your own handwritten message containing any exciting news, such as 'Last night had a ripping time.')

This rather dopey rule restricted how much you could write, but it had been the practice in most foreign countries. It all changed in 1902, when the UK led the way, followed by France the following year, in introducing what were called 'divided backs'. A divided back was what it said – the back of the card was divided in two, with the address to be written on the right-hand half and the message on the left – the arrangement that still operates

today. It instantly meant that the other side, the illustrated side, could feature a proper image, covering all the space.

At roughly the same time there were two other developments. First, advances in photographic and printing techniques meant that high-quality images could be mass-produced very cheaply. Second, the good old Post Office helped things along by allowing all postcards to be sent for only a halfpenny, as opposed to 1d. – or twice as much – for a letter inside an envelope. Thus began what is still called the Golden Age of Postcards, which lasted roughly from 1900 to 1914. Postcards themselves sold for a penny each, cheaper if you bought a set. Along with the cheaper postage, this made them irresistible. Postcards were on sale everywhere – in shops, from racks in the street, from kiosks, at the seaside, in museums,

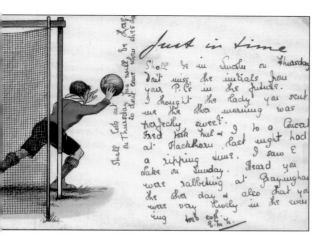

From 1894, illustrated cards started appearing. The illustrated side usually left a little gap where you could write a message.

From the beginning they were collected, which is strange in a way, that it happened at once, but they were such a novelty and also so attractive. The Golden Age is so called not just because there were so many, but also because from 1900 till the 1920s, postcards were so artistic, colourful, amusing, attractive and well produced.

Albums were sold especially to contain postcards. Women – for it seems to have been women who were the keenest collectors – stuck in their favourite cards and showed them off to their friends. In *The Standard* for 1899 there was a feature on postcards, saying that 'Young ladies, who had escaped the philatelic infection or wearied of collecting Christmas cards, have been known to fill albums with missives of this kind received from friends abroad.' It's interesting that stamps were seen as a male hobby while postcard collecting was feminine.

So what about collecting football postcards? A male hobby, presumably, but when did they first appear?

Technically, you could say that the term 'football postcard' could include a plain postcard sent by a football team, let's say Tottenham Hotspur, writing in 1888 to notify a player that he was required to turn up with his boots for a certain game. That is in one sense a football

at public events such as the major exhibitions. Almost the first thing people did when arriving at the seaside, an exhibition, a big event or when they landed abroad was buy a postcard and send it home, proving they had arrived or simply showing off about where they were.

Postcard illustrations featured every possible topic, from topographical views to portraits and angry seas to bathing beauties, and were bought in their millions. In the year 1900, 419 million cards were posted in Britain. By 1914, it had risen to 800 million.

In urban areas, there were up to five postal deliveries a day. You could send a card in the morning, arranging a lunch date, then send a card in the afternoon saying you would be late home. They did not demand much in the way of writing or punctuation skills, or stilted formal phrases – a few brief words would suffice. People immediately became addicted to them. Postcards were also extremely efficient and reliable, the most dependable means of communication, even later on when telephones had been invented. Until the 1950s, most ordinary people still did not have phones in their own homes anyway, which is why postcards, with a few blips during the two world wars, continued to be a massive industry, employing thousands and amusing millions.

Another example, circa 1900, of the illustrated side being mucked up with a message. In 1902 'divided cards' came in, allowing one whole side for the illustration.

FAMOUS ENGLISH FOOTBALL PLAYERS. 1881.

At last, a proper footer illustration covering one side. England stars from 1881, in a nice variety of strips, from football and rugby.

postcard – and they do exist, and I wish I had one as they are of great historic interest. But that is not what concerns us here. Football postcards refer to illustrated postcards within the meaning of the act I have just constituted.

As with postcards generally, football postcards started appearing from 1894 onwards, when illustrated postcards began, but there weren't many of them. As with all illustrated postcards, they really got into their stride after 1902 when 'divided' cards had taken off, allowing one whole side to be devoted to a decent-sized illustration.

Most football postcards, then and now, are photographic, and serious postcard collectors, especially of topographical cards, like to have Real Photos, which mean real photographs, as opposed to duplicated, printed versions. I am not quite sure if I can spot or understand the difference, but I am told that if you get out a magnifying glass, postcards that are not Real Photos splinter into lots of little bits, but Real Photos stay intact. To me, all photographic cards

look much the same, give or take that some seem to be clearer and better reproduced than others, which I take to mean they are Real Photos.

It is generally agreed that the first primitive photograph was taken in France in 1827. Henry Fox Talbot in England and Louis-Jacques-Mandé Daguerre in France made important advances in the 1830s, and by the 1850s you could go into a studio in Paris and have a *carte de visite* printed with your fizzog on. In 1861, according to the census, there were 2,879 professional photographers in England.

In 1888 came the first Kodak camera and in 1900 the Box Brownie, so it was approximately around the same time that picture postcards became universal that taking photographs was becoming common, though you had to be quite well off to own your own camera and to understand the complicated techniques. Ordinary people did not take their own photographs, instead relying on studios and professionals.

C. Wreford-Brown (Corinthians).

Another very early card, circa 1900, when you still had to write a message beside the illustration. Charles Wreford-Brown was a famous Corinthian.

In theory, photographic cards showing some sort of football scene were possible, and surely must have been taken, during the late 1860s. People were playing organised football and photography had been invented. Ergo, some must have been taken and cards printed, like *cartes de visite*, and handed around. I haven't found any yet. And God knows I have looked in countless car boots.

Quite a lot of photographs, as opposed to postcards, of footballers do of course exist, at least from the 1880s and 1890s onwards. They appeared in books and magazines, and prints were probably made and sold. They were even transferred onto the tops of boxes and toys, but the images don't appear to have been reproduced as postcards, not till at least a decade later, during the 1900s, which is when the passion for postcards really began.

This is one of the complications about trying to decide which are the earliest ever football postcards. A postcard showing some 1880s footballers doesn't mean it was produced in the 1880s. It might well have been printed years, if not decades, later. For example, I have a nice postcard of the Hendon Rangers Football Club circa 1890,

looking ever so casual, but it was produced as a postcard by Barnet Library in the 1960s. There is also a well-known coloured illustration entitled 'Famous English Football Players 1881', a piece of artwork that has appeared in many books over the decades, but as a postcard it was produced by the National Football Museum in the 1990s.

The earliest genuine football postcards – that is produced at the same time as the image they purport to show – date from around the same time as all other early picture postcards: the late 1890s and early 1900s.

The earliest I have is a pastel, or it could be a watercolour (anyway, artwork not a photograph), showing Charles Wreford-Brown of the Corinthians, a very famous player in his time. The back is undivided – it just says 'POSTCARD' – and leaves you the whole space on which to

One of a set of Scottish Footballers, early 1900s. David Wilson died in the First World War.

DAVID WILSON, the Queen's Park forward, learned most of his football in Langside Athletic, whence he graduated to the Hampden club. He has represented the Scottish League in their English and Irish Inter-League encounters, and also played for Scotland against Wales in 1900.

Sets were also produced showing Famous Scottish Teams of the 1900s, such as Third Lanark, now alas no longer, going 'Hi, Hi, Hi!'

The players themselves were stars in the 1890s to 1900s, but I don't think the cards were published as early as that. They came out later, probably around 1914. They have since been endlessly reproduced as they are nice little works of art.

One postcard in the Scottish Teams series shows Third Lanark, which was founded in 1868, another one of Scotland's oldest clubs, and has the headline 'Ground – New Cathkin Park'. They moved there in 1873, which could suggest that the original illustration was made not very long afterwards. By its shape and design, it does look as if it was done as a postcard. An historic card as, of course, poor old Third Lanark went out of business in 1967.

Note that all the cards mentioned so far – apart from the Hendon photograph – are artworks, watercolours or oils of some sort. Once into the 1900s, there was a torrent of photographic football cards, as there was with all postcards, as manufacturers, local and national, competed to turn out as many postcards as quickly and cheaply as possible, producing endless sets with titles like Famous Teams, Famous Players, Famous Clubs. Clubs themselves did not produce them.

British football clubs were notably dozy and superior about anything that smacked of commercialisation until well into the 1970s. They have made up for it ever since. It was left to little local photographic studios, who featured only local clubs, or the big postcard manufacturers in London or Birmingham or Yorkshire, with hundreds of artists and designers and factories producing millions of postcards every year.

For the first decades or so after 1901, the footer cards were either coloured artworks or black-and-white photographs. There were no colour photos at first. The Lumière Brothers in France perfected their colour film in 1907, but it was not available to the masses till Kodachrome arrived in 1936.

However, postcard manufacturers got around this problem by hand-tinting some of the black-and-white photos, for which they could charge an extra fee. All very useful for football historians,

write an address, while on the other side, with the illustration, there is a small space in the bottom-right corner in which you can write a very short message. It was one of the earliest series of football cards, produced in a set, for fans to collect. This one is number 2 – so it says in very small print on the bottom left (best specs out). I date it from 1899 to 1901 on the basis that divided backs were introduced in 1902.

Amongst my other early cards are two from a series on Scottish players: colour drawings showing well-known players, such as David Wilson of Queen's Park, Scotland's oldest club, and A.G. Raisbeck, a Scottish international who played for Liverpool. Raisbeck was well known in his day for playing in spectacles, though he is not wearing them in the illustrations.

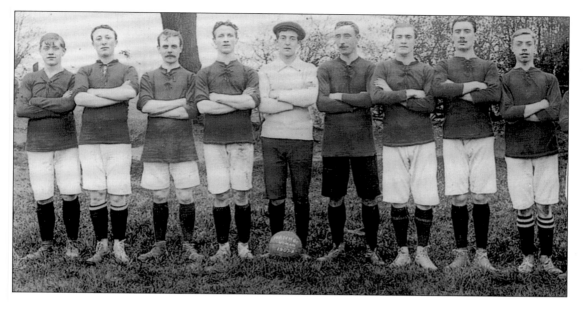

Early cards from the 1900s were often colour–tinted by hand, even minor ones. Above, the ball says they were called Ivanhoe, 1907–8, while below they were G or OS something, 1904–5.

for you can see the colour of the strips the teams actually played in. I have a postcard of a team called Ivanhoe Nomads – so it says on their ball – and in their 1907–08 line-up they are clearly wearing red shirts, so no arguments there. In a 1904–05 postcard of a team whose name appears to begin with a 'G' and an 'S' – I can't quite make it out – they are all wearing light-green and dark-green stripes. A bit faint and fading, but all the same, very natty.

On the other hand, the hand-tinting could have been done by someone using any old paints to hand, or leftovers. Historians beware.

A. G. RAISBECK, Liverpool, belongs to Stirlingshire, and is considered one of the best centre-halfs that Scotland has produced. He is a speedy and resourceful player, possessed of excellent judgment. Has represented Scotland in her Association and League Internationals. He is 5 ft. 9½ in. in height, and weighs 12 st. 9 lbs.

A.G. Raisbeck of Liverpool, who played for Scotland from 1901–7, wore specs in real life and often on the pitch – but not on pretty postcards.

Chapter Two

THE HISTORY OF FOOTBALL

Football as we know it has been around since 1863, when England gave football to the world, so hurrah for us, but football as we don't now know it has been around for, well, for ever. Kicking or throwing some roundish object around has been practised since we all lived in caves. In almost all civilisations evidence of some sort of ball-playing has been found, from China in the East to Mexico in the West. In Medieval Europe, a form of it was being played in Italy, Germany, Holland, France, England and Scotland, but the rules, such as they were, have been all but forgotten, and anyway, they varied from country to country, from village to village, from time to time.

Folk football in Britain was a pretty rough affair, usually held on the same festive holidays each year, when two teams of unlimited numbers would try to get a ball from one end of the village or the neighbourhood to the other end and reach a designated goal. Kicking each other, fighting, settling old scores, using weapons or any sort of physical violence was allowed, and people did get badly injured and, sometimes, killed.

How did this chaotic game suddenly get itself organised in 1863 and why did it happen in England when forms of football had been played for centuries in so many other countries?

The first important element revolves round the English public schools, which as an institution did not exist elsewhere in quite the same way. In the early nineteenth century, when public schools were at a relatively low ebb, with falling numbers of pupils, a new breed of Muscular Christian headmasters arrived who encouraged the playing of football to foster team spirit and also give the chaps a healthy occupation, exhaust them physically and thus distract them from any less desirable energy-sapping private activities in which they might be tempted to indulge.

Each of the big public schools, like Eton, Harrow and Charterhouse, had their own version of football, which led to slight complications when chaps moved on to Oxford and Cambridge and had to work out between themselves what was allowed and not allowed. The arguments usually centred on handling the ball (which was generally deemed OK as long you didn't run with it, for that was rugby) and hacking (which meant tackling but covered most aspects of what we could call physical assault, whether a player had the ball or not).

In 1848 a group of ex-public schoolboys at Cambridge met to try to agree on a set of rules, and apparently wrote them down, but no copy has survived and things went back to as they were before.

The meeting that mattered and finally sorted things out took place at the Freemasons' Tavern near Lincoln's Inn Fields in London on 26 October 1863. Representatives from a dozen or so clubs, the members mainly drawn from the public schools, Oxbridge, the army and the Church, drew up a set of rules that they all agreed to follow and to set up a new body called the Football Association.

Under these original 1863 rules, you could still handle the ball but not run with it, though by 1866 this had disappeared, while violent hacking was banned from the beginning, which led to some of the members at that first meeting refusing to join the FA, suspecting Association Football, as it soon became known, was for softies, not real men.

Very quickly the FA's rules were adopted by other clubs around the country – though for a while Sheffield FC (no connection with United or Wednesday), which had been formed in 1857 and is generally agreed to be the world's first football club, held onto their version of the rules, as did Queen's Park in Glasgow, founded in 1867. But within a decade or so they came into line and the FA's rules became accepted throughout the UK.

There was not, however, a sudden mad passion for football, with football mania sweeping the country, for the very good reason that at this stage it was mainly the poshos who were playing it, amateur or military types who could afford their own kit and had access to playing fields. They were not interested in attracting or charging crowds and only ever took part in a succession of friendly games. There was no competition of any sort, no points to be scored, no pots to be won (apart from winning a cap for representing your house or your school): just pride in playing the game.

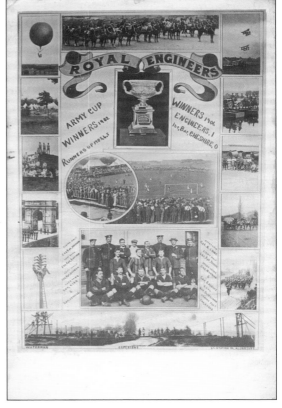

The army, plus public schools and Oxbridge, were founders of the FA in 1863. The Royal Engineers got beaten in the first FA Cup final of 1872, but went on to win many other pots.

Then in the year 1872 came two major innovations, both instigated by Charles Alcock, Secretary of the FA. The first FA Cup competition was started and then also the first international, which was held in Glasgow between Scotland and England, a game that ended in a 0–0 draw. The FA Cup was immediately very popular and attracted a lot of interest each year, but once a team was out of it, that was it: all competition of any sort was over for another year, and excitement and interest dwindled.

The real big, important changes in football took place in the 1880s and had very little to do with the public schools – which brings us to the other vital element that helps to explain how formalised

football came to be created in Britain and not anywhere else.

We were the first industrialised country in the world, the first to have vast urban areas, factories and factory workers, and also the first country to have railways, which improved all communication, enabling goods and people to be moved around, whether for work or leisure. Football was soon being taken up in these new industrial centres in the North and the Midlands, often formed around factories, workers clubs and church groups, many of the latter being run by clerics who had played the game at the public schools they had attended.

Ordinary working men playing for these Northern and Midlands clubs could not afford to buy proper gear or afford time off to play or travel to games, so an unofficial system of expenses grew up, which led to under-the-counter payments and inducements. Star players would find a nice shiny guinea in their boots after a game.

Officially it was illegal, as the FA had ordained that football should be an amateur game, but shamateurism soon spread. As a result, clubs got better, more people came to cheer them on and competition for the best players began, with good players being tempted away from rival clubs, or from 'abroad'. In the 1880s this meant Scotland, where the local players were proving to be excellent at dribbling and passing, as opposed to kick and rush, which was essentially how the public schools had played the game.

For the first ten years or so, the FA Cup had been dominated by the public school or army teams – the winners including Oxford University, Old Etonians, Old Carthusians and Royal Engineers. The army, along with the public schools, had always encouraged football for much the same sort of healthy-in-mind-and-body reasons. The Royal Engineers were in the first final and got beaten but won it in 1875. A postcard issued in 1906 shows them still winning army cups, if no longer the FA Cup.

The Hon. Arthur Kinnaird, later Lord Kinnaird, played for Old Etonians in nine cup

Blackburn Rovers in 1882 were the first non–Southern, non–public school team to get to the final of the FA Cup. Alas, they got beaten by the Old Etonians.

Harrow School, 1870–71. Two of the earliest photographs of footer
players (originals in the National Football Museum).
Just look at those stripes, feel that superiority.

HIGHGATE SCHOOL. 1st XI.
1910-11

A. Low   E. W. Meade   H. M. Read   G. R. Mackay   C. E. R. Heaton Ellis
R. R. Plaistowe   C. H. Shipton   C. A. Caslon   R. G. Mack   A. M. Ritchie
(Captain)

My oldest postcard of a public school team, Highgate School 1st X1 in 1910–11.
Not quite as dazzling as the Harrow chaps, but still pretty classy.

finals, and when he retired he became an FA official, serving as FA President for thirty-three years. In his playing days he was known for his excellent hacking, or getting stuck in, as we would call it today. There is an oft-repeated story of his mother telling one of his friends that she was worried he would come home one day with a broken leg. 'Don't worry, my Lady,' replied the friend. 'It won't be his own.'

In 1882, a team not from the South, outside the public school old boy network, managed for the first time to get to the Cup final. This was Blackburn Rovers – who got beaten 1–0 by Old Etonians. The following year, another Blackburn team, Blackburn Olympic, got to the final, again against Old Etonians – this time the OEs were beaten 2–1. Never again did an amateur team win the FA Cup. The Industrial North had arrived.

The Blackburn players were all ordinary working men with ordinary jobs, but no doubt were getting pound notes slipped their way after every game, and especially after a victory. In 1885, the FA bowed to the inevitable and declared that professionalism was legal – authorising what in effect had already become widespread. If the FA had not done so, they might well have lost control of the game and another body would have taken it over.

Once the professional clubs had to pay out regular wages every week regardless, it became

Spot the posho? Yup, left is R.N. Bosworth–Smith of Oxford University in 1895. What about those crazy socks and natty blazer.

T. McLintock, also 1895, who played for Burnley as a professional.

hard for them to find the money if they had been knocked out of the FA Cup early doors. By now, the big northern clubs were attracting gates of up to 10,000 for a good Cup game, but that quickly dwindled when it was back to endless friendlies, which were often cancelled at the last moment or had to be arranged against poorer teams.

The person credited with establishing the idea of a league system was a Scotsman called William McGregor of the Aston Villa club in Birmingham. He was worried, like many other professional clubs, to whom he sent a letter with his proposal, by the problem of attracting crowds to friendly games against often inferior teams. In 1888 a meeting was held in London, and then another in Manchester, and the first ever Football League was formed.

It is amazing, in a way, that it had taken them so long to set up something we now think of as so obvious and essential. It had been 25 years since 1863 and the formation of the FA, yet all that teams had played were friendlies and Cup games. Blame the public schools, I suppose. Taking part, playing the game, playing fair: that was the point, not all this professional nonsense and concerns about nasty things like money and point-scoring.

One good thing about the public schools during those early decades when they dominated football, and even afterwards, up to the Second World War, when amateur football remained a strong force, was that they were damn good at photographs. They hired the best photographers, used the best studios, printed the best photographs and published the best books. Some of the finest ever football books, the grandest and most lush, are those that were produced around 1900 – written by gentlemen about gentlemen and meant to be displayed in their libraries, hence the leather covers, good binding and excellent production. Once the masses arrived into football, alas, standards did rather drop, with cheap paperback books and football magazines and poor mass-market printing.

It also has to be admitted that public school chaps do take good photographs, in the sense that

Curly Hill, a folk player in Workington's annual street game, Uppies and Downies – on the winning side in 1908.

in their best togs they do look pretty special, and ever so clean and fresh, wearing the best-quality kit, and, of course, they all naturally knew how to pose and look superior.

I can find myself gazing for ages at those two snaps of Harrow School football players in 1870–71. Original copies are in the National Football Museum, but one of them has appeared as a postcard for many years. At first you think they are wearing striped pyjamas, but then you notice the boots. In one photo, the striped strips are all matching. But in the other there are two variations of stripes and also another style of cap, which has Turkish overtones. Was one of the school team and the other a house team? No doubt someone somewhere is doing research, as football history is now a little industry, probably trying to relate it to that famous photograph of Oxford's Bullingdon Club in which the young

David Cameron stars. There is a strong similarity, even though they are a hundred years apart.

I don't know if these Harrow photos were turned into postcards at the time, as I have not seen copies, but I am sure they must have been – or at least postcard-sized copies would have been run off for the team members to buy and send to their friends or to stick in their family albums.

The earliest public school team postcard I have – printed as a postcard at the time, with a divided back, which is a clue to its age – is one for Highgate School 1st XI in 1910–11. They are not quite as alarmingly superior and effortlessly relaxed as the Harrow players, but all the players are named on the front of the card, under the photo, which is a great help.

All public school and Oxbridge football teams from this and later decades always look so obvious – you can tell them a mile away, not just because of their top-class kit and upper-class demeanours, but also because you can usually spot cloisters, or similar, in the background. Individual portraits of early public school players, playing perhaps for

Oxford or the Corinthians, are equally distinctive. Their breeding shines out.

Once professional football got into its stride, the top professional clubs and players were having their photographs and postcards printed just as frequently as the amateurs, but somehow you can still tell the difference. R.N. Bosworth-Smith, ex-Harrow and -Oxford, appears in the same publication – *Famous Footballers*, published in 1895 – as T. McLintock, who played for Burnley. The former looks every inch a posho, with his blazer and sleek hair, while the latter, though neat and smart, looks somehow a little rough.

Not as rough, though, as Curly Hill, one of Workington's folk footballers, part of the rabble who played uppies and downies through the street. He is obviously feeling pretty chuffed, not to say superior (despite his baggy pants and torn shirt), having presumably won a game in 1908, holding up the ball as evidence and having his photo taken and a postcard printed as proof for posterity of his great achievement.

Spurs players, 1935, in their chunky training jumpers and ample shorts, greet a new signing, Duncan (right), from Hull City.

Chapter Three

FAMOUS FOOTBALL CLUBS

here were just 12 clubs that formed the first Football League in 1888. All true fans should be able to recite their names like a litany, or at least have worked out codes and systems for remembering them in the long hours of the dark night when you can't sleep so you let your brain try to recall them, hoping that before you have completed them you will finally have dozed off. The famous twelve were: Accrington, Aston Villa, Blackburn Rovers, Bolton Wanderers, Burnley, Derby County, Everton, Notts County, Preston North End, Stoke City, West Bromwich Albion and Wolverhampton Wanderers.

All of them were professional clubs, not amateur or Oxbridge. Six were from Lancashire and six from around the Midlands. Note the lack of any London or even a remotely southern club. One reason for this was that there was a still a strong feeling of anti-professionalism in the South, a belief that football should be played by amateurs. Also note the lack of any north-eastern clubs, an area today we look upon as one of the heartlands of football, or any from Yorkshire.

It is interesting that all of these twelve clubs are still in business, one hundred and twenty years later – even if one of them, Accrington (or Accrington Stanley as they became from 1891), has had a chequered history, falling out of the Football League in 1960 and returning to the FL fold in 2006. Over half the original 12 were still in the 2009–10 season top division, the thing we now call the Premier League.

They kicked off for the first time on 8 September 1888, with two points being awarded for a win. It took them several weeks, with the season in full swing, to think, 'Hold on, heh up: what if it's a draw, surely that deserves something?' It was then decided that a draw should earn one point. That first league was won by Preston North End, who went all season unbeaten and became known as the Invincibles.

In 1892 a second division was created, again with no Southern teams, unless you count Lincoln City and Grimsby, though a year later Woolwich Arsenal joined the Second Division. Two years after that the Southern League was established,

Preston North End, the Invincibles, won the first Football League and the FA Cup in 1888 without losing a game or conceding a goal. Beat that, Barcelona.

for mainly London-based professional clubs, which for a time was considered as important as the Football League. But eventually all the leading London and Southern clubs who were good and professional enough opted to play in the Football League.

In 1920, the Football League split into three divisions, with sixty-six clubs in all. A year later, the Third Division was split into North and South. In 1958, the League was restructured into First, Second, Third and Fourth divisions and expanded to include 92 teams, which is the number we have today (at the last count, anyway).

Another thing to observe about those twelve original founding clubs of 1888 is that they did not contain one of what in recent years we have been referring to as the Big Four – Manchester United, Chelsea, Arsenal and Liverpool – the clubs that everyone had assumed, until 2010, would always be, for ever and ever, at the toppermost of the tops.

The Big Four's two northern clubs – Manchester United and Liverpool – did enter the Football League not long after it began. Man U made it in 1892 as 'Newton Heath' (not becoming Manchester United till 1902) and Liverpool a year later, in 1893. But after that, for many decades, they had fairly undistinguished histories, with several demotions as they moved between the First and Second divisions. As late as 1974, Man U were still lingering in the Second Division. Liverpool also had their ups and downs, not finally leaving the Second Division till the 1950s.

Chelsea crept into the Second Division in 1893 and made it to the First the next season, but for decades they were another up-and-down team, not emerging from the Second till the 1950s.

Arsenal were also a late arrival, not making the First Division till 1911, but since then, unlike the other three, they have always been members of the elite, a quality team, one of nature's aristocrats, which is what they still like to think they are today. Most of the time (he said through gritted teeth), Arsenal have continued to be a team of class and quality.

What all this shows, if anything, is that, first, almost all English clubs have been with us for a long time, surviving far longer than other institutions that were also formed at the end of the nineteenth century. It illustrates the enduring nature of football and how it has become part of the fabric of society. Second, it also suggests that the same teams will not be at the very top for ever – or so we hope.

If you look at any newspaper from the 1900s, at the league tables or match reports, you will recognise the name of almost every football team in every one of the football leagues, for almost all are still going strong, if not quite in the same leagues, or with the same distinction – but at least half of the shops, department stores, firms and companies and brands then being heavily advertised have disappeared. Despite our present worries about the financial positions of so many clubs, they do seem to struggle on, survive bad economic times, keep going regardless of whichever chancers or dodgy characters have taken them over. The supporters, and the local communities, help keep them alive and turn up to cheer them on, even when there appears little worth cheering or supporting.

But there is a general feeling around today that it's too late, so much wealth has been gathered by the few, that the same lot *will* now continue to dominate for ever and no one else will get a look-in. It is true that money does appear to be able to buy success, but on the other hand we have had clubs in the past who appeared to be mega-rich moneybags who had the resources to buy any players they liked. For a while in the 1930s, Sunderland were known as the 'Bank of England Club', while Blackburn Rovers in the late 1990s suddenly had a massive amount to spend, but it was all relative to what other clubs had and didn't last long. Will this time be any different? Will Chelsea and Manchester City, currently blessed with unbelievable resources, succeed with all their money – and keep all their money? We shall see.

The moment the Football League was established in 1888 it totally dominated English football, and then all football, as other nations soon adopted a league system and became obsessed with league tables and ups and downs.

Scotland's FA was established in 1873, just one year after that first international, while the Scottish League was founded two years after the English one, in 1890, and consisted of ten clubs – Dumbarton, Rangers, Celtic, Cambuslang, Third Lanark, Hearts, Abercorn, St Mirren, Vale of Leven and Cowlairs. That's how they finished, in order, in the first table, with Dumbarton and Rangers being declared joint winners after a play-off that ended 2–2.

Of those ten clubs, Rangers and Celtic are still going strong, as are Hearts and St Mirren. Dumbarton have rather tumbled down the leagues, while the others, alas, have all but disappeared. I must admit I had never heard of Cowlairs till I looked up that first league table of 1890. They were based in the Springburn district of Glasgow, but they dropped out of the league five years later, in 1895.

A national football league had national focus and was followed every week of the season by people all over the country, which was a godsend for postcard manufacturers. A firm in London could knock off endless series of postcards, making sure they included the current top teams in both England and Scotland, plus, at a pinch, Wales and Ireland, knowing they would sell all over the country.

Some of the early well-known top teams – such as Preston North End and Blackburn Rovers – had been captured in coloured drawings or touched-up photographs from the 1880s, which appeared in magazines. But they were not at first produced as picture postcards, not till at least around 1900, when mass-market postcard production began.

Two of the earliest sets of footer postcards, 1911, produced by a magazine, *Health & Strength*, famous for helping young weedy lads become hunks.

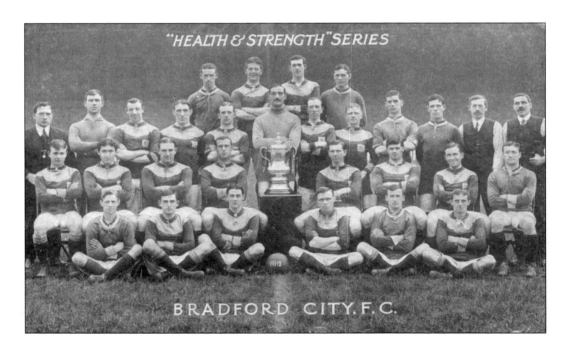

One of the first sets of pictorial postcards of famous teams is reckoned to have come from Raphael Tuck, about the biggest name ever in postcard production, based in the City of London. They issued a set called Celebrated Association Football Clubs in the 1902–03 season.

I have used the word 'reckoned' as postcards, unlike stamps and coins, do not have an exact history. Stamps and coins were controlled from the beginning, being more or less official and government-produced, and the details of each issue were carefully recorded and documents kept. Hence stamp and coin collectors have proper catalogues, such as Stanley Gibbons for stamps, in which they will find listed all stamps ever issued and will know, with certainty, that these records will be correct.

With postcards, even the biggest manufacturers did not keep proper records (or they were lost, went up in smoke during war-time bombing), and from the beginning there were also scores of little local firms and photographers all over the country cashing in on the craze for football postcards, most of whom didn't last long and who didn't always number or record their products. So there might well be lots of cards we still don't know about. However, Eric Krieger, who in 1983 produced the first attempt at a definite account of football-postcard manufacturers, *Good Old Soccer*, believes that Tuck were probably the first to produce sets of footer cards.

There were only six teams featured by Raphael Tuck in that first set, carefully selected to give a regional balance. Newcastle United were chosen from the north-east, Everton from Lancashire, Bristol City from the south-west, and Aston Villa and Small Heath (who became Birmingham City in 1905) from the Midlands. For the London area, they ignored Woolwich Arsenal (still in Division Two) and Spurs (who were in the Southern League) and chose New Brompton, who later became known as Gillingham.

Other major manufacturers quickly followed, or might well have come out around the same time, with their own sets of famous teams, including Wrench Ltd, C.W. Faulkner & Co.,
the Rotary Photographic Company, the Rapid Photo Company and Valentine and Sons from Dundee.

There was one successful producer of football postcards in the 1900s who himself was a footballer – Albert Wilkes, who played for Aston Villa and England. He trained as a photographer, for most footballers had had another job before becoming a player, then when he retired ran his own studio in West Bromwich, producing cards of the leading teams and players until his death in 1936 (though the business continued till the 1960s).

One of the earliest sets of football cards produced by a magazine – a trend that became enormously popular later on – was issued by *Health & Strength* in 1911. This was a magazine devoted to physical fitness and the body beautiful, founded in 1898, which told you how not to be a seven-stone weakling in three easy lessons or how to put on two inches in a month with their wonder methods. It had regularly featured footballers and their diet and health regimes, and then began producing a series of postcards of the leading English, Scottish and Irish teams. They were not giveaways as such but instead sold as ordinary postcards that you were meant to post in the usual way, as the reverse side has 'Halfpenny Stamp Here', but above the photo of the team there was the headline '*Health & Strength* Series', thus giving themselves some useful advertising. The first teams were from the 1910–11 season and on the back of the postcard it named all the players, such as on the card showing Bradford City, winners of the FA Cup in 1910–11, and the Glasgow Rangers team of the same season. I do like cards where all the players are named. So helpful.

Some cards included even more fascinating facts, such as some produced by R. Scott of Manchester. In their card of the Everton team in 1906, it lists on the reverse side not just all the players but also the weight and height of each. They were so small in the 1900s, not one over six-feet tall, even the goalie, but they were ever so chunky, mostly around eleven stone.

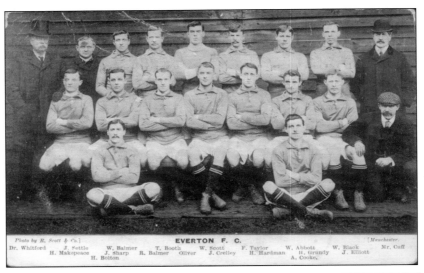

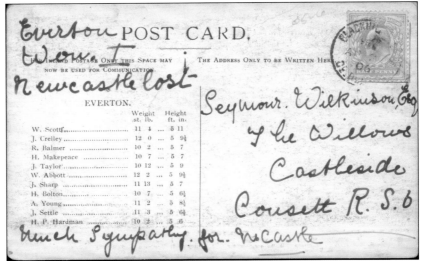

Thanks to R. Scott of Manchester for this Everton team of 1906.
On the reverse it lists weights and heights. Gold dust for any true fan.

R. Scott were photographers and printers and had been producing sets of football teams in small booklets from as early as 1900 – thus giving us the problem of having to differentiate between football photos and football postcards. The booklets were just to be kept and treasured, and it wasn't until about 1903 that they started producing postcards of football teams, printed to be posted in a postcard format, though, of course, many of them were kept and never posted.

As competition intensified between all the rival producers, there was a move to tart up some of the basic team photographs with fancy lettering or borders, or adding a rose, leek or thistle as a decoration to signify an English, Welsh or Scottish series.

There was also a vogue for cut-outs, taking mug shots of the players and arranging them in a montage, which was a good way of shoving in players from different seasons perhaps or when

ENGLISH INTERNATIONAL TEAM.

As competition increased between postcard manufacturers, decorative touches were added. A rose, circa 1910, indicated the England team.

you didn't have access to the official team shot. Clubs themselves did an official team photo at the beginning of every season, and large framed prints were hung in the boardroom while postcard versions were sold locally to the fans. The official Spurs photo for 1913–14 shows not just the whole squad but also trainers, officials and the team doctor.

The leading amateur clubs, like the Corinthians, also appeared on the early cards, as of course they were household names in football circles. Leading local clubs were also featured in cards produced by local photographers, such as the card of the Ilford team of 1905–06, produced by Crosheher and Howard, Publisher, Ilford, or so it says on the back. Ilford, founded in 1881, was once one of the more famous of the amateur clubs. This photo was taken in 1905, presumably to celebrate joining the Isthmian League, where they remained for 61 years, appearing in the last Amateur Cup final in 1974. They sold their ground and merged with Leytonstone in 1979.

Those who are gone, football-club-wise, tend to get forgotten very quickly by the next generation, though if they have been taken over by another club or changed their name, such as Woolwich Arsenal becoming Arsenal or Thames Iron Works turning into West Ham United in 1900, then keener fans are usually still aware of the ancient names. If they have died a quick and sudden death and not had a transplant and survived in another body, the chances are only true football anoraks will know they ever existed.

It was interesting in 2010 that a group of Man United fans started a protest group and turned up at home games wearing green-and-gold scarves and shirts. I was confused when I first noticed them, wondering why, as Man United fans, they were not wearing red. Green and gold were the colours of Newton Heath, formed in 1878, a team of railway workers who later turned into Manchester United. This campaign group intended to wear the old colours instead of red as a protest against the current American owners of Man United, who they alleged had stolen the soul of the club, borrowing millions in order to buy it,

Using mug shots, done in a montage, meant photos could be used from different seasons, long before computer wizardry.

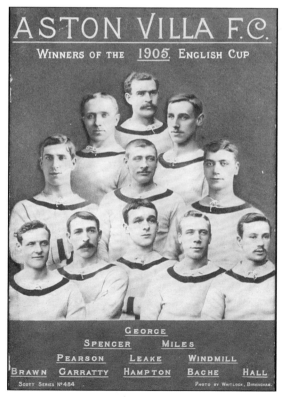

ASTON VILLA F.C.
WINNERS OF THE 1905 ENGLISH CUP

GEORGE
SPENCER   MILES
PEARSON   LEAKE   WINDMILL
BRAWN GARRATTY HAMPTON BACHE HALL
SCOTT SERIES Nº 484   PHOTO BY WHITLOCK, BIRMINGHAM.

It was unusual for footer postcards to feature reserves, trainers and anyone wearing a boater, but Spurs in 1913–14 lined them all up.

Ilford FC in 1905.

Ah, Clapton Orient in 1920–21, of blessed if rather distant memory. So named because many of their players were employed by the Orient shipping line.

then loading it with the debts and massive interest payments.

One of the advantages of postcards is that clubs and teams live on if they were in the League at some point, as every League team always got itself photographed.

It is, of course, hard to track down postcards of the really old ones, such as Blackburn Olympic, the first provincial club to win the FA Cup. Having achieved all that, they became football's first major casualty. They made it into the League but survived only one season and were wound up in 1893, having been eclipsed by Blackburn Rovers.

Other early League clubs who achieved some sort of glory but didn't last long include Darwen FC, who were credited with being the first club to be quasi-professional, albeit illegally at first. They were in the League from 1891 to '99, then disappeared. Then there were Wigan Borough, New Brighton, Bradford Park Avenue, Leeds City, Durham City, Loughborough, Burton

Swifts and Burton Wanderers. The last two were both in the League at the same time in the 1890s, making Burton the smallest English town to have ever boasted two league clubs.

The postcard I am always looking out for is one showing Middlesbrough Ironopolis – what a name to shout after you've had a few jars. They made Division Two in 1893 but were gone by 1894.

Clapton Orient, another long-gone club, were clearly very popular at one time, judging by the numbers of postcards still around. Their programmes are particularly desirable. They were founded in 1888 and named Orient because many of their players were employed by the Orient shipping line. They got elected to the Football League in 1905 when it expanded to 40 teams and survived as Clapton Orient till 1946, when they were subsumed into Leighton Orient, then became Orient, then back to Leyton Orient again, which is where they are now, I think. Oh, it can be confusing, collecting footer postcards.

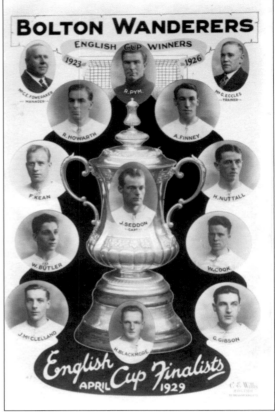

In 1926, Clapton Orient surprised the nation by defeating the mighty Newcastle United in the fifth round of the FA Cup.

Another League team, now totally gone, was called Thames, based in London's East End. They survived only two seasons as a League team, 1930 to '32, till they were chucked out and replaced by Newport, the only London club so far to lose their League status. In a game against Luton in 1930 Thames attracted a crowd of only 469, still said to be the lowest ever crowd for a Saturday-afternoon match in the English league. So they have not been quite forgotten.

Two good examples of the photo montage, cutting out mugs and arranging them nicely.

Above left: The Barnsley card, 1907, was produced by 'Irving, Photographer'.

Above right: Bolton Wanderers, who beat Portsmouth 2–0 in the 1929 FA Cup final.

Chapter Four

H. GAL...   A. JAMES   ...DEAN

FAMOUS PLAYERS

The first players who found their fizzogs on postcards, photos, books and magazines were the public school players, naturally enough, as it was their game and they had access to decent photographers and classy printing techniques. They were national heroes, players like C.B. Fry and G.O. Smith, to the football-following public as a whole, people to look up to, admired by the couth and not so couth.

It was a bit like those boarding-school stories in the comics and children's books that dominated the reading material of boys and girls right up until the Second World War. The vast majority of people didn't go to boarding school, had no experience of them, probably didn't know anybody who did, but stories about them were lapped up and did not seem to arouse dislike or envy. In fact, most readers probably wished they were at Greyfriars or Green Gables rather than their own scruffy school down the street. So the public school footballers, however remote they might have been from everyday life and experience, were role models who looked and behaved and played the game the way everyone thought it should be played.

C.B. Fry was a famous cricketer as well as a footballer of the 1890s who went on to have a sports magazine named after him, which he edited and wrote for, just as many years later did Charles Buchan, who played for Sunderland and Arsenal and England in the 1920s. (The excellent *Charles Buchan's Football Monthly* ran for many years and later became *Goal*.)

G.O. Smith – full name Gilbert Oswald – another star of the 1890s whose image appeared everywhere, played for Oxford University, the Corinthians and England. He also played cricket, but when he wasn't doing either that or playing football, he was an author and headmaster. As a footballer, he was described as the finest player of his generation – the soccer equivalent of W.G. Grace. 'A genius in football,' wrote C.B. Fry about G.O. Smith; 'he was as straight a shot as I have ever seen, except perhaps only Steve Bloomer of Derby County, on one of Steve's special days. G.O.'s was every day.' Bit of a backhanded

C. M. BUCHAN IN ACTION.

Left: Charlie Buchan, 1920s Sunderland and Arsenal star, went on to edit his own magazine.

Below: Billy Meredith, of Man Utd, 1920s, chewed a toothpick while playing.

It is fairly hard to find good postcard versions of them because postcards of single players, as opposed to team shots, were not as popular and did not sell as well. Football fans, after all, have always followed clubs rather than individual players, who in the nature of things, then as well as now, do tend to move on whether or not they have made a show of kissing the club badge. (Not that I think they did such things in those days; in fact, not till very recently in football history. Emotion was kept to a minimum. If you scored a goal, you might get a handshake from the captain, then you went quietly back to your position. None of that kissing and cuddling and similar nonsense.) Also, the shape of a postcard did lend itself to a team shot – not too small that you couldn't make out each of the eleven players and it was cheap enough to mass produce.

compliment to Bloomer, who was a professional and, as perhaps his name might suggest, not one of the silver-spooned quality.

Another famous Corinthian was Charles Wreford-Brown (see the illustration of him in Chapter One), who is always credited with inventing the word 'soccer'. While he was a student at Oxford, he was asked one day if he was going to play rugger. He said no: 'I am going to play soccer.' There was a fashion at the time for shortening words and adding 'er' at the end, and apparently he took the word soccer from Association Football, though it seems a bit of a tortuous shorthand.

The photographic portraits of these early amateur stars usually appeared in books first, then postcards later, and were of excellent quality. There were also lots of drawings and caricatures done, rather amateurishly but nicely hand-tinted or watercoloured. Once the professionals took over, the star players were even more celebrated and their faces appeared on the sports pages and in the popular football magazines, but the quality of their images was not quite as good.

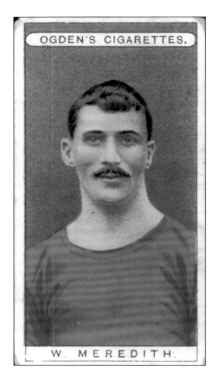

OGDEN'S CIGARETTES.

W. MEREDITH.

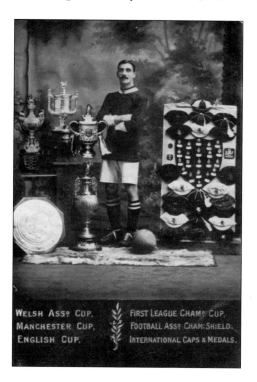

The earliest cigarette cards to feature footballers was a set produced by Ogden's in 1896, and from then on millions and millions poured out. It's estimated that between 1900 and 1930 there were 10,000 different sets printed – just with a football theme. They were therefore in direct competition with postcards for football fans, boys and adults, who wanted to acquire images of their football heroes and favourite clubs.

Every player in every League club in England and Scotland who turned out for a League game between 1900 and 1930 was immortalised on a cigarette card somewhere at some time, while images of the big stars were endlessly recycled.

The two best-known professional players of the pre-First World War era were Steve Bloomer (born 1874) of Derby County and Middlesbrough, and Billy Meredith (born 1875)

The smallness and neat shape of cigarette cards were more suitable for mug shots and far more of them were published. Portraits of celebrated players from the 1900s to the '20s are therefore easier to find on cigarette cards than postcards, though many of the manufacturers tended to use the same basic photograph, touching it up and cropping it to suit their own purposes – and presumably to avoid paying a fee to the original photographer. Disgusting.

Cigarette cards arrived in the 1890s, around the same time that professional football was attracting mass audiences, and the idea came from America. They came free as long as you bought a packet of cigarettes, which most people did. They were seen as a vital marketing tool in the battles between the rival cigarette manufacturers. Adults bought the packets and small boys hung around them, begging for any cigarette cards that might be inside. 'Got any fag cards, mister?' was a cry echoing down most high streets. The manufacturers went for topics they knew would be popular with boys, such as soldiers and sportsmen.

"DIXIE" DEAN

A. JAMES

H. GALLACHER

Stars of the 1920s to '30s (from left to right): Dixie Dean of Everton, Alex James of Arsenal and Hughie Gallacher of Derby County and Scotland.

of Manchester City and Manchester United. They did appear on many postcards, as they were so famous and had won so much, but also on thousands of fag cards.

Bloomer, despite C.B. Fry's catty remark, was a remarkably consistent striker, getting twenty-eight goals in twenty-three games for England and three hundred and fifty-two goals in five seasons, making him the leading scorer each season. He wasn't the traditional bullet-headed centre-forward, which was the way most strikers were at the time and how they usually looked on cigarette cards and postcards, but rather thin and weedy, known as Paleface. Arsenal would certainly have snapped him up today.

Meredith, who was Welsh, went down the pits at 12, till all the English clubs started chasing him. He was the first winger, but not the last, to be known as the Wizard of the Wing, a position most recently held by Ryan Giggs. In newspaper drawings and caricatures of Meredith you can tell it's him if there is a bit of wood sticking out of

his mouth. He sucked a toothpick, even when on the pitch, which he explained originated when he was a miner and used to chew tobacco. Fans would send him toothpicks, just like Beatles fans would send their heroes jelly babies in the 1960s. In photographs, he smartened himself up.

In the post-war years, Dixie Dean – Tranmere Rovers, Everton and Notts County – was mega, a true phenomenon, setting scoring records that are unlikely ever to be beaten. In the 1928–29 season at Everton he scored 60 goals in 39 games. Beat that Didier, Fernando, Wayne or whoever is currently knocking them in.

There was also a clutch of Scottish stars, usually undernourished-looking waifs who did magic on the wings, most of whom spent their careers in England, such as Alex James (The Wee Wizard), Alan Morton (The Wee Blue Devil) and Hughie Gallacher, who was one of the legendary Scottish team who beat England 5–1 in 1928 and became known for ever, at least in Scotland, as the Wembley Wizards.

In the late 1930s, and in the years just after the war, the big star was Stanley Matthews of Stoke City and Blackpool. He made his debut for Stoke at seventeen and made his final League appearance, again for Stoke, just five days after his fiftieth birthday. Again, that seems a record for an outfielder unlikely to be beaten, yet we are supposed to be in an era when health and diet and fitness have never been better. Matthews must have appeared on millions of cigarette cards and postcards, as there were hundreds of individual sets in which he featured, though sometimes it is hard to believe that it is Matthews as the printing is so rubbish or has been horribly touched up. I have about six different images of a 1920s Spurs star called Fanny Walden and in each one he looks totally different.

The player you can always spot, even in the most crowded team shot, is Billy Foulke, known as Fatty Foulke from a very young age. At 19, in 1894, he first stood between the posts for Sheffield United weighing 19 stone. By the time he had moved on to Chelsea, he was 22 stone. He was made captain of Chelsea, was adored by the fans and turned out, or at least lumbered out, twice for England. He ended his career at Bradford City, his weight now up to 25 stone. In his retirement he appeared on Blackpool beach saving penalties for pennies. He caught a chill in 1916 and died aged only 42.

Some of the best football cards were produced in the 1930s by *Topical Times*, a popular football magazine. Their black-and-white ones were excellent, done in various sizes on stiff cardboard, so you could have posted them, and were well reproduced – but their colour ones are laughable. I keep sets of them just to make myself smile. They touched up the originals, giving fans the benefit of seeing the true colours of their teams' shirts and socks, such as Sunderland in vivid red-and-white stripes or Portsmouth in deep blue, but when it comes to the faces, the colours run, the eyes look weird and the players look altogether mad.

I also treasure a card of a 1920s star in red and white, this time the colours of Stoke, called H. Davies. On the back of the card, it says he moved on to Huddersfield and played for them in the 1930 Cup final against Arsenal. It also says, 'Is a keen billiardist with some three figure breaks to his credit.' I tell my children that oh yes, I was a famous footballer once, about 80 years ago.

Fanny Walden of Spurs, 1920s, appeared on loads of cards, yet somehow managed to look a bit different on each.

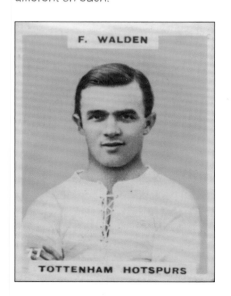

W. J. FOULKE, the burly goalkeeper of Sheffield United, is remarkably smart between the sticks. He can take shots from all directions, and is very clever in clearing his lines. Probably the biggest and heaviest player in British football. In 1897 he played for England against Wales.

Billy 'Fatty' Foulke, 19 stone with Sheffield Utd.

Now and again postcards of players in civvies were produced, but usually for special occasions, such as them all setting off on an overseas tour or on top of an open-deck bus during a victory parade or attending a civic reception. The Bolton Wanderers team, winners of the first FA Cup final held at Wembley in 1923, were caught in their best suits before going into Bolton Town Hall for a slap-up do. They are all in three-piece suits (though some of the waistcoats look suspiciously like cardigans), their collars are pinned at the neck to display their ties and at least one is wearing spats.

Spats were quite a common fashion item for men up to the Second World War, worn over the ankle and shoe to protect against splashes of mud. The Portsmouth manager Jack Tinn was famous in football for having a pair of lucky white spats, which in 1939 he wore during their FA Cup run. He insisted they had to be fastened for him before each game by Pompey's winger, Fred Worrall. It seemed to work. Pompey got to the final – and won.

Towards the end of the 1930s a lot of 'letter cards' were issued featuring footballers, taking

Left to right: H. Davies of Stoke (no relation) and two *Topical Times* cards in gruesome colour: A. Beasley of Arsenal and B. Nieuwenhuys of Liverpool.

Not often you see the stars in civvies: Bolton Wanderers, 1923 Cup winners, outside the Town Hall after a victory reception, in best suits and spats.

the idea from the fold-out letter cards on sale at the seaside showing different views of the resort. These were printed in a strip, which then folded flat and went inside the letter card, which you then posted. You could buy Twelve Famous Soccer Stars, which shows mug shots of twelve players, all of whom played for London clubs – two each from Arsenal, Spurs, Chelsea, Fulham, QPR and West Ham – so I assume this set was on sale in Brighton or Southend, where Londoners went on holiday. Another set, this time just of six players, was called Six Famous Football Stars in Action and included, inevitably, Stanley Matthews of Blackpool. Both sets were produced by Sporting Mirror Publications of London EC4.

All these star players of yesteryear, right up until the 1950s, appeared on millions of postcards and other sorts of cards that must have made fortunes for the manufacturers and publishers without the players getting a penny. In those days, they had no agents or lawyers to control their images.

All footballers, stars and otherwise, could have done with the extra money as even in the First Division, playing for a top team, they were earning little more than double what a normal skilled workman of the period was getting.

In 1901, the maximum wage for a professional player was set at £4 a week – less in the summer months. In 1910, it rose to £5, then in 1920 to £9, creeping back down again to £8 two years later, at which it remained even after the First World War, when a full League programme returned and crowds were enormous.

In 1951, the maximum became £14 a week; then in 1958 it rose to £20 a week. In 1961, after a long, hard battle, the maximum wage was abolished. Until then, all those great players, all household names in their day, their faces known and collected by the millions, never made more than £20 a week during the whole of their playing careers.

RON ROOKE, Arsenal F.C.   L. DUQUEMIN, Tottenham F.C.

E. DITCHBURN, Tottenham F.C.   ARCHIE MACAULAY, Arsenal F.C.

R. THOMAS Fulham, F.C.   ROY BENTLEY, Chelsea F.C.

BOWIE, Chelsea F.C.   BEDFORD JEZZARD, Fulham F.C.

J. W. YEOMANSON, West Ham F.C.   C. HATTON, Q.P.R. F.C.

G. POWELL, Q.P.R. F.C.   R. DICK, West Ham F.C.

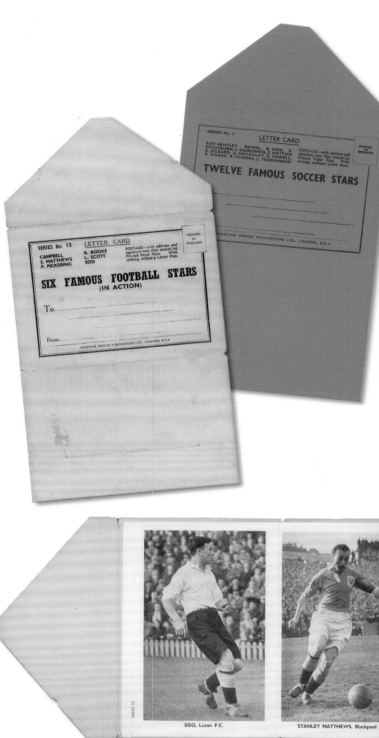

SERIES No. 13   LETTER CARD
CAMPBELL   R. ROOKE
S. MATTHEWS   L. SCOTT
P. PICKERING   SOO

SIX FAMOUS FOOTBALL STARS
(IN ACTION)

To

From

LETTER CARD

TWELVE FAMOUS SOCCER STARS

SOO, Luton F.C.   STANLEY MATTHEWS, Blackpool

The theory behind a fixed wage was a leftover from the good old amateur days and the Corinthian spirit of the Victorian era, which many of the FA officials had been brought up with. It assumed football should be played for fun and that to make money the master would ruin football for ever. It was also thought that a maximum wage imposed on all clubs would keep things fair and equal, stopping clubs tempting away the best players from rivals. All clubs would therefore have an equal chance. Despite the maximum wage, this didn't really work. Players, naturally, wanted to play for the best, most successful clubs and there were always ways to tempt them, with underhand payments and inducements.

The same attitude was felt towards transfer fees. There was no cap on them, but always a lot of tut-tutting from the blazers and the old farts of the FA whenever a player was transferred for more than washers. In 1900, they did try to limit transfers to £10, which they thought reasonable, but pulled back from making it mandatory and so transfer fees gradually crept up to £400.

And then in 1905 there was a sudden and colossal jump when Alf Common was transferred from Sunderland to Middlesbrough for the then astronomical sum of £1,000 – the first ever four-figure transfer. 'That's it,' they all thought, wringing their hands, 'football will never be the same again, the game has been ruined, money has truly taken over.'

Alf Common was a small, tubby, bustling Geordie, 13 stone but only 5ft 8in. high. Sunderland had bought him for £350 from Sheffield United just a year previously, who were therefore pretty annoyed that Sunderland had made this sudden huge profit. Middlesbrough wanted him because they were desperate to avoid relegation, and the first game Alf played in, which always seems to happen in football, was away to Sheffield United. Alf scored from a penalty. Boro stayed up. It was money well spent, so they all declared.

Transfer fees then crept up almost every year: not always for a famous player, often for a journeyman who was seen at the time as a vital purchase. Who now remembers Danny O'Shea, the first £2,000 transfer, who went from the Southern League to West Ham in 1912? But David Jack, who cost £10,000 when he went from Bolton to Arsenal in 1928, was a star, as was Tommy Lawton, who became the first £20,000 transfer when he moved from Notts County to Chelsea in 1947.

Opposite page: 1930s letter cards – you bought them in strips inside a letter card, which you could then post to a loved one.

Below: 1930s stars from a letter card, 'Six Famous Football Stars', published by Sporting Mirror Publications.

RON ROOKE, Arsenal F.C.   P. PICKERING, Chelsea F.C.   LAURIE SCOTT, Arsenal F.C.   CAMPBELL, Charlton F.C.

Another star in civvies, looking a bit menacing: J.B. Butler of Arsenal, said to be the best half-back of 1927–29.

Jack and Lawton were Celebrated Footballers, just as 40 years earlier Meredith and Bloomer had been Celebrated Footballers, judging by the titles of the series of postcards that were issued using their features. And they were, of course, seen in footballing households and in the nation generally, especially at Cup final time, when the country came to a halt and was bombarded with images of the two teams and their leading players.

Star players were not, however, like today's footballing celebrities. Their few perks were modest, such as giving them a cushy job in the club office or promising them a rent-free club house, and they remained strictly in the social and cultural setting from whence they had come. They were seen as other ranks while the directors were officer class who lived in different social strata.

Professional players still went to training on the bus, lived in ordinary streets and had the same sorts of holidays. No security guards or minders accompanied them; no paparazzi hid in bushes outside their gated private estates to capture them or their lovely wives. They didn't get invited to posh parties or Mayfair nightclubs, or have the theatre and movie stars of the day dying to meet and mix with them, or the prime ministers invite them to Chequers or be seen photographed with them.

About their only freebie took place at the local variety theatre on a Saturday evening, when, if their team had won, they got free tickets, were invited on stage, cheered loudly and given free beer and probably (though this, of course, was never mentioned) got a chance to meet the chorus girls afterwards and boast about their sporting prowess.

They were strictly working-class heroes who knew their place and stayed in it, hoping, if they made a bob or two, to have enough to buy or rent a sweetshop or a pub. Most, though, after their careers were over, went back to the same humble job they had had before so-called fame had been thrust upon them.

Chapter Five

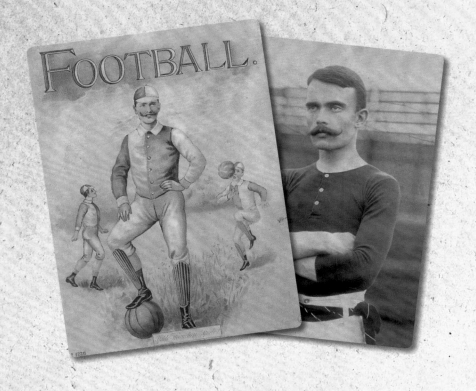

FOOTBALL GEAR

One of the many joys and pleasures of football postcards is that you can literally see football changing and developing. A postcard can look old because it is faded, sepia-tinted, has old-fashioned lettering, but it can also look old because of its contents – if you can spot them. You do need good eyesight, possibly a powerful magnifying glass and a rough idea of the history of football equipment and football laws, but with a bit of practice you can roughly date a football postcard from what the players are wearing and doing.

On the other hand, you can just say, 'Hmm, that shirt looks cute, like that collar, I do think there was something reassuring about a good pair of knickerbockers, what a shame you don't see those socks any more, must have been hell in those boots,' then move on to the next fascinating chapter.

Shirts were any old colour in the very early days, back in the 1860s, and it was the colour of your cap that identified you or your team, but by the first Cup final of 1872, teams had settled down to having their own distinctively coloured shirts. They tended to be very bright, heavily patterned and influenced by the public schools and their house colours – like those magnificent young men in their flying Harrow strips.

Working men played in their ordinary working clothes at first, but as they got more professional, they copied the shirts and shorts of the public schools. On the whole, our famous teams have stuck, more or less, to what we now accept as their traditional colours for the last 100 years, but in the early years, the colours and designs were sometimes not the same as they are today.

In the postcard of the Liverpool team of 1905–06, who won the First Division title that year, they seem to be wearing two-tone shirts – with a sort of top bit, round the collar, a darker colour than the rest. As the postcard is in black and white, it's hard to be sure what the colours were, but presumably one of them was red, which was what they wore from 1896.

Real experts on the precise history of their own clubs can usually date postcards to within one

LIVERPOOL F. C.

[Manchester.

Photo by R. Scott & Co.]

Top Row—W. Connell, *Trainer*   J. Hewitt   C. Wilson   S. Hardy   M. Parry   E. Doig   W. Dunlop   J. Hardy
Second Row—R. Robinson   J. Gorman   D. Murray   J. Hughes   A. Raisbeck   J. Cox   G. Fleming   S. Raybould   A. West
Bottom Row—A. Goddard   G. Latham   J. Carlin

Choir boys? No Liverpool 1905–06. Their colour was red by then, but they appear to be in two-tone shirts. The goalie wore the same as the rest, plus cap.

year, depending on the style and design of the shirts and any badges or fancy bits, even when the photos are in black and white.

We do know that Everton were wearing an all-black strip in the 1880s, before they settled down with blue. In 1903, the Scotland national team was not wearing dark blue but primrose-and-white hoops, the racing colours of Lord Rosebery.

Arsenal's red shirts with white sleeves did not appear till 1933, when their manager, Herbert Chapman, decided to make them more distinctive. Until then their shirts had been all red, which they had originally copied from Nottingham Forest, who had kindly given them a set of their shirts when they were starting up in Woolwich in 1886. They also gave Arsenal a ball, always very useful.

The material of the early shirts was heavy wool or flannel, and there was a wide variety of patterns – spots, dots, stars, stripes, squares, hoops. Around 1905 or so, the designs adopted by most League clubs settled down into plain or stripes, giving up

the fancy bits and patterns, though quite a few opted for hoops or halves, and a handful or so persisted with sashes or Vs.

The design of the neck is always worth examining. They came buttoned like old-fashioned vests, with or without collars, straight necks or laced up, or with a bit of string hanging out, which you were supposed to pull once you had the shirt over your head. Books for boys often advised cutting the ends of the laces so they did not get in your eyes. Lace-up collars remained one of the most popular styles until the Second World War. They recently made a return for one-off games when clubs were celebrating some sort of centenary, or at least celebrating how to sell more repro strips.

The first shorts were white, a bit like cricket flannels, then developed into knickerbockers made of wool or fleece, which were tied below the knee. In 1904, the FA was affronted when Charlie Roberts of Manchester United was seen to be hitching up his knickerbockers during a game to make them shorter – 'Disgusting, what will people think?' – but it was a fashion amongst players that had begun to catch on despite the FA's reprimands. Within another year, long knickerbockers began to fade out and a shorter version came in – which naturally were known as knickers. For short.

Postcards showing players wearing knickerbockers, whether professional or amateur, indicates the period was some time pre-1906, or thereabouts. They were still pretty baggy, right up to the 1930s, and still known as knickers, the term always used in football programmes. Alex James, of Arsenal and Scotland, was always mocked for his incredibly baggy shorts, but he was thin and weedy and seems to have imagined they made him look bigger and stronger.

Goalkeepers wore the same shirt as the rest of the team until 1909 – as you can see in that 1905 Liverpool postcard – which can make it difficult to identify who was the goalie. One sure way to pick them out is by their cap, which they almost always wore, even for the team photo.

Above: Arsenal, 1937–38, in red with white sleeves. Till 1933 they wore all red, having borrowed their first shirts from Notts Forest.

Below, left to right: Well-dressed 1930s players: Vic Woodley of Chelsea, W.E. Houghton of Aston Villa, George Antonio of Stoke City.

Above left: Give us a V: Joe Bradford, 1920s, Birmingham.

Above right: Or halves: J. McKinnell, Blackburn Rovers.

After 1909, the FA decreed that goalies should wear red, blue or white jerseys. In 1912, green was also allowed and this became the most popular colour with goalies. Up to the Second World War, goalies' jerseys were always heavy and woollen, and always known as jerseys because they were so heavy. They had polo necks, which you could roll up or down if and when the weather got tropical.

Numbers on shirts, from one to eleven, were introduced for the Cup final of 1933 and in 1939 became compulsory. They were very useful for spectators. Each side was numbered one to eleven and you always knew that number nine was the centre-forward, while number eleven was the left-winger. Now the numbers are pretty meaningless and can range from one to one hundred and eleven. By the time you have taken in all the numbers, they've been transferred.

Belts were very popular in the early days and most players wore them up to about 1900. They went with knickerbockers, helping to keep them up. They came in many thicknesses and varieties,

broad and thick or thin and tassly. J. Graham of Millwall, in his 1895 portrait, looks a little bit girly with his stripy belt tied in a bow and probably wouldn't make the Millwall team today, though he was renowned as a tough full back who was a good header of the ball. Broad belts were, on the whole, more popular, helping to make players look tough and manly, as if they were about to lift weights or pull horses.

Boots were strong enough to kick horses, or other players, with thick leather bits at the toes and ankles like armour plating, and they continued like this right up to the 1960s, though some avant-garde players, like Stanley Matthews, had started to adopt so-called Continental boots, which real men dismissed as slippers, as early as 1953. He had first seen them at the World Cup in Brazil in 1950 and acquired a pair for himself.

What the well-dressed goalie was wearing. Unknown player and team on a card, posted 1905.

which of course was rarely necessary in the days of gentlemen players. When the game got more professional and serious, referees were given sole charge, and by 1891 a referee and two linesmen had replaced umpires. In 1893, the Referees' Association was founded.

The first known use of a whistle, as blown by the referee, not a spectator, was in 1878. This would be very handy in dating postcards, if, of course, you could properly see the ref or a whistle. Crossbars came in in 1874, replacing a bit of tape, so look out for them. Goal nets were introduced for the Cup final of 1892. They are much easier to spot.

Markings on the pitch are often very hard to identify, but they were slightly different in the early days, particularly around the goal area, which was in the shape of a bra, not a rectangle, until the 1901–02 season. Look carefully in early cup final photographs, if you can find them, and you can usually spot the strange curves.

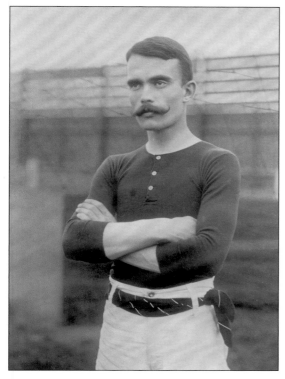

J. Graham of Millwall, 1895. Goodness, how standards at Millwall have slipped since they gave up sashes and curled 'taches.

Studs: now there's a study in itself, but postcards don't help as footballers rarely hold their boots up to the camera, thus depriving posterity of another vital clue. There was much argument amongst FA officials in the 1860s, when they began sorting out the rules about boots, before deciding what length studs should be, what sort of materials should be used and should they be in bars or individual studs.

There were many changes of the rules in the early years, but it is not always possible to spot any studs in contemporary photos, unless you can blow them up.

Referees were known as umpires at first, as in cricket, and each side brought along its own umpire, who stood at the side and shouted or waved his handkerchief to attract attention if he saw an infringement. A referee was someone who arbitrated between teams if it got heated,

Another splendidly dressed player, circa 1890, with shin pads worn outside. German, name and team unknown.

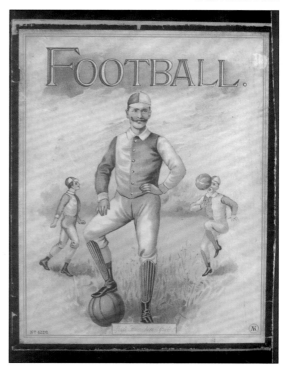

Shin pads, invented in 1874, were worn outside socks till around 1900, so you know these fine chaps must have been pre–1900. Kent Army team, 1895.

Shin pads or shin guards are an invaluable tool for carbon, I mean, football dating. Shirts and shorts, socks and boots were, after all, in existence before football came along and were adapted to football's needs as the years progressed, but shin guards were a purely football invention – and we know who invented them and when. It was a Nottingham Forest player, Sam Widdowson, who first wore them in 1874 and they were soon adopted by all teams and players.

For about the next 25 years, till around 1900, shin guards were worn outside the socks – as you can see in the team shot of the Kent Army in 1895. The coloured illustration of that fine gentleman in a dinky hat and natty shin guards is actually German, from around the 1890s. It was originally a design on the top of a German toy box and was later turned into a postcard.

From 1900, shin guards became thinner and less bulky and were shoved inside the socks, where they have remained to this day.

Balls were a bit like medicine balls up to about 1900, and if you peer hard you can see they had sort-of ends, at least a patch at the north and another at the south. In the postcard of the very smart-looking unknown team (on the opposite page), you can clearly see the ball – held on the front row – has a little patch at the end. This particular team are ever so snazzily dressed but not exactly uniform, as they appear to be wearing an assortment of knickerbockers and different shirts, one of which looks suspiciously like a knitted jumper, as if his mum had done it for him.

Looking smart was certainly not exclusive to the professional teams. The two unknown players standing together, whom I take to be brothers, are displaying some very interesting

Unknown rural team, 1900s. Very well dressed for country lads,
even though all the shirts don't quite match.

period gear, such as the belts, white knickerbockers, shirts with a sash across – a style that lasted for a few decades – and also a ball with ends.

The ball eventually lost its medicine-ball appearance and became stitched in panels, put together like a jigsaw so there was no end. You still had a lace where the inner bladder, having been blown up and inserted, was secured inside. You tried to avoid heading the ball at the lace bit, unless you wanted to lie down for a bit and recover.

The size of the ball was standardised from 1872 onwards, the maximum circumference being between 27 and 29 inches when fully blown up. They were not really heavier than they are today, despite what many people think. Being made of leather, without any plastic coating, they just became heavier in bad weather as they absorbed moisture and mud.

Dubbin: whatever happened to dubbin? Everyone up to the 1960s had to have a tin of dubbin handy to smear over their balls and their boots to try to keep out the rain. However, one need not feel sorry for a football-equipment manufacturer, then or now, for what a marvellously lucrative one hundred and thirty years they have had.

Football gear, obviously, did not exist till we had football, nor did the race of hacks known as football reporters have any occupation or anywhere to go on Saturday afternoons, so there are millions of folks all over the world who are very grateful for the invention of football.

The earliest advertisements for football equipment that I have in my collection date from the 1880s, even before professionalism was legally allowed. The range of boots, shirts, belts and balls is enormous. Tens of thousands of people were soon employed in the factories and in retail shops up and down the country.

Looking at an 1888 catalogue, I see that goalies' gloves were on offer, which had what look like pimples to give a better grip, very much the same as today, but ear guards for players, alas, never caught on. They would have been handy today when the manager comes to the edge of his technical zone and screams at you.

In 1902, at a time when club shirts and designs were still changing and evolving, Manchester United and Liverpool both backed a proposal to end the confusion over all the different shirts and the eye-dazzling, distracting designs. Why not, they suggested, decree that in all League games, the home side should always wear red and the away side wear white. Now wasn't that a simple, sensible solution? Almost communist and utterly utilitarian.

Arriving late at a game, you would always know instantly which was the home team and which the away side. Watching on the telly (though it hadn't been invented), it would also be very clear, though possibly not in black-and-white telly days. Young fans would only have to learn 'Come on You Reds' or 'Come on You Whites' and none of those other more complicated chants. For hundreds of years, cricketers, after all, had only ever played in white, so why should footer be much different?

Fortunately for all those manufacturers of repro shirts and club shops everywhere currently making millions from craven fans, this 1902 suggestion was never adopted. Just as well really. Half of the romance of football is knowing and following and loving your club colours. Kissing is optional.

Two unknowns, possibly brothers, 1900s, with natty strips. Even local teams splashed out on proper gear, which was great news for the kit manufacturers.

Chapter Six

CROWDS

Around 2,000 people turned up to watch that first international between Scotland and England in Glasgow in 1872, which was pretty good for a first attempt. It was helped by the fact that the whole of the Scottish team came from the Queen's Park club, Scotland's oldest, and they played at a local ground, the West of Scotland Cricket Club in Partick. The club were so pleased by the turnout, at one shilling each admittance, that they pressed Glasgow Corporation to let them have a bigger ground – which is how they then came to take over Hampden Park.

Roughly the same number turned up that same year in London – also at a cricket ground, Kennington Oval – to watch the first Cup final, then most rushed off to watch the end of the Boat Race, being varsity chaps. The following year, kick-off time for the Cup final was brought forward to mid-morning, so chaps could watch the Boat Race without having to rush. It was almost the first time that a kick-off was altered by the authorities to suit themselves, long before Sky TV came along.

During the 1880s gates for big games, in the Cup and then the League, reached around the 10,000 mark, then went up to the 20,000 mark in the 1890s, but the phenomenal gate that astounded the whole world came in 1901 for the Cup final, now being held at Crystal Palace. The attendance was 110,820 to see Spurs play Sheffield United. Spurs were still in the Southern League, which in itself was remarkable, but it was also a classic North–South battle, which always helps. This massive attendance, and the huge crowds gathering weekly for League games, established football as a popular sport enjoyed by a mass following, on a par in public consciousness and participation with the theatre and the music hall, until then the only other leisure pursuits for which large numbers of people paid to watch.

That 1901 Cup final is about the first game where postcards exist that show the crowd, as it was so enormous, though in fact the postcards were not printed (by W.H. Smith) till a few years after the game. The spectators didn't have much comfort or many facilities, being herded on to

Brighton—Sheffield cup tie, 1922, taken by local snapper Tom Wiles,
who set up his camera and a board with his name on, did crowd shots,
printed postcards and sold them to the fans.

grassy banks and kept back with ropes. I have one postcard (not shown) that shows an incident during the game, which the unknown photographer was pretty smart to catch. It is captioned 'Man Hurt' and shows a Sheffield United player being attended to. Alas, you don't see much of the crowd, but I think the match took place at a Bolton Wanderers ground for the replay. The Crystal Palace game ended in a 2–2 draw, but Spurs won the replay 3–1.

Photographs of crowds were hard to take with cameras of the day, and anyway, why would you want to take photos of fans when it was the team people were interested in, whose images they wanted to see and cherish? The newspapers did photograph the crowd for cup finals, as part of their stories of the big event, but most of the main manufacturers of postcards were not interested.

There is an early postcard, circa 1910, of some players running out onto the pitch, being led by the captain, presumably, wearing a very low-slung belt – but I have failed to identify the team, or the ground. On the back it says the postcard was printed in Liverpool. At a guess, it could have been

Goodison Park, but again there is not much to see of the stadium, though the crowd is quite clear, most of them young men in caps.

It was often left to little local postcard producers to realise there could be money in crowds. In the early 1920s, a Brighton photographer called Tom Wiles used to set up his camera and a board and photograph the crowds before kick-off at Brighton and Hove Albion games, then playing in the Third Division. He would go round the crowd, doing sections at a time, then display his results at postcard shops all over the town centre the following week. The idea was that if people could spot themselves in the crowd, they would buy a postcard. On a board he would write his name and address, so everyone would know who he was and what was going on. He carefully captioned the postcards with the date and game. He also included a number, usually held up on a board, so the fans would know which card to ask for. It was a smart ruse, providing a unique document of local social history. A major postcard firm would not think of covering such an event as sales would be so small. I presume that other equally enterprising local photographers, all around the country, had similar wheezes.

Studying these 1920s postcards of crowds carefully, you are first of all struck by the hats. Everyone seemed to be wearing one. It illustrates that flat caps were the badge of the working man all over the country, not just in the North, as many suppose. Bowlers were worn by foremen or people in more managerial positions. In the '20s, the racier, spivvier, younger types favoured trilbies, or in the summer months perhaps a boater.

What is really surprising, though, is the number of women in the crowds, when you consider how packed and uncomfortable it was, shepherded together in the open air, subject to language and shouting, which ladies were supposed to shelter themselves from. In earlier cards only occasionally can ladies be seen, but by the 1920s, post the Great War, they were more common. They are still only a small minority, and you have to peer carefully, but at that Albion versus Sheffield cup tie in 1922, you can definitely spot a few women in rather jaunty berets dotted around. They might have gone with their husbands or boyfriends, though they appear to be on their own, not linking arms or even standing close. Were they lone fans who

Crowd scene at Watford, 1920, taken by Harry Cull. Admire the caps, trilbies and the odd female fan.

Another Brighton crowd scene, January 1931, game unknown but taken by Wiles of Brighton.

had gone on their own? Women at football games is usually reckoned to be of recent history, after grounds went all-seater and civilised, but from the beginning, as newspaper reports have shown, there were always quite a few female fans.

Some of them might have been poshos, possibly wives and daughters of directors, which is what I suspect the women in the fashionable hats were in the grandstand of a postcard published in Southampton by A. Rapp, Marine Photographer. The date appears to be 1911, though that might well be just a number, and I can't make out what the other lettering means, nor the big painted letters W.O.R. Was it part of an advertisement or the name of the club or ground? Such a shame I can't work it out because the faces in the crowd are so clear, the women in their smart hats so cheerful.

Fans dressing up, painting their faces, wearing exotic outfits for big World Cup matches, knowing they will be seen on telly all over the globe, is nothing new – apart from the fact that in the old days they did it purely to amuse themselves. It always happened at FA Cup finals, ever since the 1900s, especially amongst Northern supporters coming to London for their big day out, possibly the only day in their lives they would ever come to London, so they wanted to make

Charity Football Match, 8th March, 1905

the Cup final. Winston Churchill was presented to the England and Scotland teams before their match in 1941, part of the effort to boost wartime morale.

Charity games, which meant that the gate money went to charity, go back to the 1900s. Miss Lil Hawthorne kicked off a charity football match on 8 March 1905 and it looked a very jolly event, judging by the postcard that commemorates it – the only problem being that it doesn't state where it took place or who played, but presumably it was in Bristol, as it was published by Ozograph Limited, St Michael's Hill, Bristol. It looks like a proper stadium, either Bristol City's or Bristol Rovers's, both long-established professional clubs.

Miss Hawthorne was huge at the time, a singing star of music hall, variety and pantomime. She was a native of Texas but came to London in 1898 to appear in the West End with her sisters. She stayed on and toured all the big provincial halls in the UK till she died in 1926. In March 1905, she was presumably delighting the theatre crowds in Bristol. Did other stars from the show come and help her kick off that day? Or it could have been that some of the players put on fancy clothes, along with their boots?

On a smaller scale, I have a postcard of a pretty small crowd watching a woman in a long skirt and hat kicking off a game in what could be a public park. What looks like a telegraph pole on the left must be a clue to the situation. Oh, it's so annoying when people don't date and place their cards properly.

There was a strong connection between football and the music hall in the Edwardian era. Both were major spectator sports, both appealed to the working industrial classes and their stars tended to come from a working-class background. They

it a proper fun day and dressed up accordingly. Alas, not many photographers turned these scenes into postcards, although in Barnsley several local publishers produced amusing cards starring Amos the donkey, which was the mascot of Barnsley FC in the 1910s, surrounded by Barnsley fans, most wearing silly hats and big rosettes.

Games being kicked off by well-known personalities go back a long way, many of which may have had some sort of charity element. Politicians and royals often kicked off big games like cup finals, showing they were in touch with the people, even if they had never been to a football game before. The first royal visit to a game was in 1909, when George V attended a Scotland–England game, then in 1914 he went to

GOAL!

Above right: Another charity kick–off, but star and venue not known.

Below right: Colchester players with fans, 1920s, taken by J. Stutter, Photographic Artist, Colchester.

understood each other, feeling sympathy for each other's causes. They were both keen on their rights and each fought campaigns for union acceptance.

There had been early attempts in the 1890s to start a footballers' union, though the bosses had managed to suppress it, but in 1907 the Professional Footballers' Association was finally formed in Manchester, with Billy Meredith in the chair at the first meeting.

However, the music-hall stars were still enormously better paid. While a top footballer in the 1900s, despite playing for England and being a household name, his face on thousands of postcards, was still on £4 a week, a music-hall star like Marie Lloyd or one of the leading comics was on £100 to £150 a week. Music-hall stars did therefore quite like to help out football clubs, by kicking off a game or inviting them to their shows.

There was a famous music-hall show that incorporated a football theme – and starred the young Charlie Chaplin, who was then appearing in Fred Karno's so-called circus, which was a touring variety show with sketches, not an actual circus. It toured the major provincial towns from about 1906 to 1909 and was entitled the 'Football Match'. Depending on which town they were in, the football references would be to the local teams.

My friend Eric Krieger, who has researched the show when it appeared in Oldham in 1909, still with Chaplin, who was now getting star billing, says that the plot, such as it was, revolved round an attempt to bribe Stiffy, the goalkeeper, to throw a game. There was a football-crowd background painted on a backdrop, but holes were left for real faces and up to 100 local extras were often hired when they got to the big finale, which was the Cup final. Sounds great fun. Wish I'd seen it. The notion of any footballer being bribed to throw a

game was and is, of course, preposterous. Could never happen. Could it?

Postcards showing real fans at real games are always interesting, especially when some of the fans have surrounded the players after some pot-winning exploits. They are spur-of-the-moment shots, not posed, when the players are dirty and exhausted but triumphant. I have one postcard that on the back says it is the work of 'J. Stutter, Photographic Artist, Colchester', which I presume shows the Colchester United team having won something, though the pot displayed is pretty puny. You see the bandages and mud and bruises, but the photographer has persuaded them to attempt the traditional pose, with the front row sitting down. One player has got lost in the crowd,

Players with fans, this time outside the stadium, date and place unknown, but someone did manage to drag out some chairs.

while officials are getting in on the act and at the back the fans are pressing to get into the picture.

I have several other postcards of players with fans around them, but alas few clues as to where and when they took place. In one, a team with striped shirts appears to be outside the ground, as you can see an entrance marked 'Grandstand 9*d*., Ladies, Boys'. By the look of it, it must have been a League club of some sort, big enough to hire a helmeted constable to control the throng and a trainer/doctor figure to carry a medical bag. Someone had the presence of mind to go and fetch some wooden chairs for the front row to sit down on, but I wonder why on earth the photo was taken outside?

In another, rather faded photo of a team with fans and some sort of trophy, someone has put an arrow on a figure in a waistcoat standing behind the players, and on the back, in handwriting, it says: 'Beverly Football photo, 1907. Dad is at back.' It's a proper postcard with 'Postcard, Inland Correspondence, Address Only' printed on the back, so some photographer must have run off copies, hoping both players and fans might buy them.

Grounds were literally grounds at first, pieces of open, flat ground where a game could be played,

though in the case of public school grounds, the grass was cut and cared for, with some sort of changing-room where the chaps could get changed in privacy. Professional grounds in the 1880s were not much better at first, with a hut to get changed in and the crowd kept back with ropes, but as they were professional and admission was charged, they had to erect some sort of barrier all the way round the pitch and provide some sort of cover for the directors, often a dinky little grandstand, as at a horse-racing track.

By 1900, with crowds now in the thousands, proper purpose-built or purpose-converted stadiums had started to appear, the earliest ones being Everton's Goodison Park, and Celtic Park and Ibrox in Glasgow. Massive earth-moving equipment was moved in to create raised embankments around the pitch, thus giving a better view, with crush barriers to stop everyone falling forward at an exciting moment. The typical stadium had one grandstand and three sides of open terracing.

A Scotsman called Archibald Leitch (1866–1939) is usually credited with being the first stadium architect, though he was in fact an engineer by training. The Ibrox disaster of 1902, when 26 people were killed after some raised

More players with more fans. Arrow points to 'Beverly Football photo 1907. Dad is at back.'

wooden terracing on which spectators were standing collapsed, was not blamed on him and his career went from strength to strength.

By 1908 he had created in Glasgow what were the three largest grounds in the whole world – Celtic Park, Ibrox Park (home of Rangers) and Hampden Park (owned by Queen's Park but also home of the national team). They were essentially vast, open, oval-shaped bowls with one main grandstand.

My oldest stadium postcard is one of Hampden for the Scotland–England match of 4 April 1908. You can see the bowl shape and the smart main stand, but the open terraces where tens of thousand of fans are crammed together look frightening. How did they not get suffocated? How did most of them see? Outside there are more fans queuing, yet there is no room left inside, only on the slopes facing the wrong way. The wall around the ground makes it look like some Stalag prison camp – brutal and scary. The game ended 1–1 and the crowd was estimated at 121,000, the largest ever for an international.

Leitch also built or worked on many of the major stadiums in England, such as Anfield, Old Trafford, Hillsborough, Stamford Bridge, Ayresome Park, Roker Park and Craven Cottage, but the shape of these was more rectangular. He was fond of fancy facades with classical overtones on the grandstands. His corner pavilion at Craven Cottage, once common at many grounds, is now a listed building, as is the old facade on the main stand at Ibrox.

In the next stage, in the 1920s and '30s, some of the open terraces then got covered, in theory, with a new big roof jutting out over them so the club could boast 'room for 40,000 under cover', but you were still exposed to the elements on all the other sides and, of course, the vast majority of fans still had to stand.

Wembley Stadium, which became the best-known stadium in the world, was opened in 1923 and was part of the British Empire Exhibition of 1924–5. Lots of postcards of it were produced and sold to the millions who visited the exhibition. In many of them you can see not just the stadium

International Football Match : Scotland v. England Hampden Park, Glasgow, April 4, 1908

Newcastle United Football Ground

Above: Hampden Park, 1908, Scotland versus England before 121,000, the largest ever crowd for an international.

Below: Newcastle United's St James' Park, 1900s.

itself, but also all the other buildings that at one time surrounded it. The stadium was only one of about twenty pavilions, exhibition halls and other attractions that were meant to show the world the glories of the British Empire after a long and debilitating war.

All the buildings were later demolished or sold off and carted away. Only Wembley Stadium remained, in isolated glory, with its Twin Towers a symbol of English football and recognised by fans everywhere – until it was knocked down and in 2007 replaced by the modern version.

Wembley Stadium, when it hosted that Cup final of 1923, was seen as a wonder in itself: 'the greatest arena in the world,' so the match programme boasted; 'the latest, most comfortable, best equipped and holds more than 125,000'.

A lot more than that turned up to see West Ham play Bolton Wanderers, storming the gates, charging in. It is estimated that somehow around 210,000 spectators got in, still the unofficial record for any British game. Kick-off was delayed and fans spilled onto the pitch, many fearing for their lives – but remarkably there were no casualties. The hero, according to the newspapers, was PC Storey on his white horse, Billy, who managed to persuade the crowds to move peacefully off the pitch so the game could begin. Bolton won, 2–0. There is one really dramatic postcard that shows the crowds from the air, looking like ants, spilling

Above: Wembley Stadium, 1923, also showing all the other buildings which were part of the Empire Exhibition.

Right: Wembley's Twin Towers, Tuck's Oilette, 1923. 'From the terraces and towers,' so it says on the back, 'are seen enchanting views of the Exhibition.'

Bird's—eye view of Wembley, 1923, and the estimated 210,000 crowd.

Action: unreal, but as seen on a pretty card, posted 1906.

Above left: Lord Mayor's Cripples Home game, 1907, produced for charity, and above right, staged goalmouth drama, 1930s.

Left: Stanley Matthews in real action, 1943.

over the pitch, with thousands still outside – a piece of national news, not just a football postcard.

Action is what, of course, all fans come to see, and while newspaper photographers were able to give us blurry-looking shots of a game in progress from around 1900, the quality was rubbish and postcard manufacturers by and large ignored action on the pitch. They resorted, as many newspaper and magazines of the time also did, to drawings or artwork of action, recreating goals or important incidents. There were also many series of action postcards that were meant to be instructional, all done as artwork, showing you how to pass the ball, take a free kick or score a goal. Postcards don't really lend themselves to

action because of their size, and even today, when cameras are so much better, you don't see many postcards of goals or incidents. That's left to telly and the back pages.

But some real-life action postcards do exist from the 1930s, showing some pretty phoney-live action, with players being tackled and hamming up their falls like a modern diver. There is a well-known card of Stanley Matthews playing in 1943 for the RAF, which does at least look realistic.

I have one action card from as early as 1907 that is remarkable for its contents if not the quality of its reproduction. It shows some young players on crutches in a goalmouth scramble and the caption says it was taken at the Lord Mayor's Cripples Home at Alton, Hampshire. There are no spectators apart from someone with a nasty-looking bulldog, so who would have wanted to buy copies, apart from the players taking part? The clue is on the back – Queen Alexandra League. Presumably the card was sold to raise money for the Home – the first example, perhaps, of a charity football card.

Chapter Seven

WOMEN

Perhaps those women in the crowd postcards were in fact football players? Look back at that photo on page 70 and they do appear young and fit, in the traditional sense of the word. Could they have been footballers themselves and not just followers of football?

Today, women's football is a massive sport all around the world, but most people assume it is a recent innovation, unaware of how and when it all began.

The British Ladies Football Club was formed in London in late 1894. The president was the youngest daughter of the Marquess of Queensbury, Lady Florence Dixie, who had been one of the earliest female war correspondents, during the Boer War. The secretary and captain was Miss Nettie J. Honeyball. In a leaflet advertising the club's first game, she gave her

Nettie Honeyball, captain of the British Ladies FC, 1894, in full football gear, including boots and pads. She organised the first women's footer game.

THE LADY PLAYER

The fellows are anxious, it would seem,
To have a game with the ladies team.

A FAST PLAYER.

The girls are quick in getting past —
In fact a few are rather "fast."

address and invited 'ladies desirous of joining the club' to write to her. As with the early years of the men's game, many of the women came from the upper classes, perhaps the sisters or daughters of those who had begun the game 30 years earlier and had now seen how much it had grown.

Their first game was held at Crouch End in North London on a Saturday afternoon, 23 March 1895, between what was called the North and the South – similar to the early men's games in the 1870s, when games were billed as Scotland versus England, even though all the players, on both sides, lived in London. In the case of the women, the 'custodian' of the Northern team, that is the goalie, according to a report of 27 March 1895 in *The Sketch*, had come all the way from Glasgow. The trains were much better in those days. It's presumed, though, that all the others came from the London area, chums of Miss Honeyball – captain of the North team – and Lady Florence.

Greetings cards, 1920s, with saucy remarks about women players. Printed in Germany by E.A. Schwerdtieger, sold in London and New York.

I have only recently discovered contemporary photographs of those two 1895 teams, and I can stare at them for ages. The North team is particularly immaculately turned out, though the South team is smart as well, which would suggest they must have been well-off gels to have afforded all the right gear, including matching strips, the latest (if alarming-looking) shin guards – worn over the socks, which confirms the date – good-quality-looking boots and heavy knickerbockers. The North are in what appears to be dark, heavy, long-sleeved blouses, possibly made of canvas, with a white stripe down the front, while the South are in slightly frillier shirts, with what could be some sort of scarf round the neck, and the design is halved, like a Blackburn Rovers strip.

I now know, thanks to that contemporary *Sketch* report, that the North were in bright red while the South were in blue. The reporter says they all wore dark knickerbockers or divided skirts. I had thought at first they were all in knickerbockers, but now I look again, a couple at the sides are in skirts.

'They certainly made a pretty picture,' writes the reporter, whose initials are given as S.D.B. and who I presume was of the masculine persuasion. 'It was an astonishing sight,' so he wrote, 'train loads of excited people travelled from all parts and the respectable army of carriages, cabs and other vehicles marked a record in the history of Football.'

Some ten thousand turned out to watch the game and were charged one shilling each. There is no suggestion in the leaflet that it was done for charity, so the newly formed British Ladies Club, all 30 of them, who had been training twice a week for the previous few weeks, must have been thrilled by the gate and the boost to their coffers.

Alas, according to S.D.B., they were rubbish:

> *As exponents of the popular winter pastime they had not the slightest qualification to take the field. The first few minutes were enough to show that football by women is totally out of the question. A footballer requires speed, judgement, skill and pluck. None of these was apparent on Saturday. For the most part, the ladies wandered aimless over the field at an ungraceful trot. I do not wish to appear uncharitable, but candour compels the statement that the experiment is scarcely likely to be repeated. Let not the British Ladies misconstrue the enormous attendance into a sign of public approval. These people had attended purely out of curiosity. Now that the novelty has worn off – its only charm – it must be clear that girls are totally unfitted for the rough work of the football field. As a means of exercise in a back garden it is not to be commended. As a public entertainment, it is to be deplored.*

The first ever women's game, North versus South, took place in Crouch End, London, in 1894. The women were immaculately dressed, the 10,000 spectators highly delighted, the press decidedly critical.

God, the girls must have been in tears when they read that report – though it's not really any worse than those many male football teams have had to put up with. For about the last 40 years, I would say the Spurs team has mostly been wandering aimlessly around the field.

Above: Stakeford Married Ladies, 1921, looking a bit, er, rough after a hard game for charity.

Below: A jollier group with natty hats, nicely posed but not named.

However, it did not kill off the desire by women to play football, even if there is no record of any other games in the London area over the next few years attracting such crowds. But playing the game did spread around all parts of England and in Scotland, where Lady Florence organised charity games. Women took their football seriously, just as they did their bike riding, seeing it as empowering, giving them some freedom, in a way part of the suffragette movement, which was attempting to give women more equality in another sphere.

Meanwhile the men's game continued to go 'tut tut', saying it was not natural, should not be allowed, along of course with those men who went along for their own amusement to see women in fetching outfits running about. There was a brief attempt at mixed games – women playing in a male team – but the FA banned this in 1902.

It was the First World War that created the big breakthrough. Over one million women went into the munitions factories, replacing the men away at the front. In the factories they began their own clubs, which included playing football, first kickabouts in their breaks, as the men had done, then organising games on Saturday afternoons against women from other factories. From 1916 onwards, there are reports of women's football clubs being established in industrial areas all over the country, particularly in the North.

On Christmas Day 1917, ten thousand people turned up to watch the women from a Preston factory called Dick Kerr – named after the two men, W.B. Dick and John Kerr, who began the factory – play another team of women. They hired Deepdale, Preston North End's ground, for five pounds and all proceeds went to a local hospital.

Dick Kerr Ladies – sometimes with an apostrophe added – became the best-known women's team and continued to play long after the war was over, as did many other of the factory teams, sometimes changing their name from the name of the factory to the name of their town. Postcard manufacturers, not to miss a trick, issued postcards of the leading teams, which were on sale all over the country.

Dick Kerr Ladies appeared on lots of postcards with different line-ups. In one of the ones I have, which includes a female trainer holding a towel, on the back in handwriting it says 'Sheffield, Yorks. Really enjoyed myself at Hillsborough, Sheffield Wednesday's Football Ground. Match between Atlanta Ladies and Dick Kerrs Ladies team. Dick Kerrs winning 4–0.' Could Atlanta have been a touring team from the USA? Possibly.

Women as fans – or were they
mums, wives, subs, trainers or
even players? 1930s postcard,
no date or names, alas.

Left and middle:
Two postcards of the famous
Dick Kerr Ladies. Attracted
a crowd of 53,000 in 1920 to
Goodison Park – then in 1921,
the rotten old FA banned
women's football.

More women as fans, 1930s – perhaps directors' wives?

The almost–as–famous St Helens Ladies, who played Dick Kerr at Goodison Park, 1920.

ST. HELENS FOOTBALL TEAM.

Posted in 1905 by a woman called Dorothy in Billericay, with a handwritten message on the front saying 'Kick-off – 1 a.m.'

Also posted in 1905 to Ethel Clarke in Market Deeping. Both cards were women writing to women.

Another postcard has a printed caption: 'The Famous Dick Kerr's International Football Team', which was true, in that they played the French ladies football team in April 1920, when the French girls were touring England, attracting crowds of up to 25,000. Dick Kerr Ladies made their own tour of France later that year.

You can also find postcards of ordinary factory teams, not quite as professional-looking as Dick Kerr. In fact, some look a bit rough and ready, as if they have just come off the night shift. As Oscar Wilde said: 'Football is all very well as a game for rough girls, but is hardly suitable for delicate boys.'

Not all of these minor ladies teams, as with the men, have included their name or year on the postcard, but on the back of one rather, er,

plainly dressed ladies team it says in handwriting: 'Stakeford Married Ladies – played on 5 May 1921 in aid of Distress fund.' Stakeford is in Northumberland, so it could have been in aid of a mining disaster. If the team was for married women was there also a team for singles?

It is interesting to contrast some of the rather rougher-looking factory teams of the 1920s with Miss Honeyball's well-dressed, classy teams of 1895 – just as it is to compare the smooth, elegant chaps in the 1870 Harrow team with the working-class teams who came 30 years later.

Women had also become camp followers, supporting the men's teams, appearing in the team pictures, travelling with the team, possibly even playing with them, judging by two postcards

WE LOVE TO SEE A GOOD HALF BACK.

MAKING UP FOR THE OTHER PLAYERS.

Artist Fred Spurgin had fun at women's expense in the 1920s – and sold loads of cards.
Note that the women are playing with men, which the FA did not allow.

WHAT'S THE GAME? KISS OR KICK?

A FINE ALL-ROUND PLAYER.

WELL PLAYED LADIES—HOW ABOUT **SWAPPING SHIRTS**!

A more modern Bamforth card, 1970s, with a much used joke.

showing women standing with the men, but perhaps they were just wives or girlfriends.

On 26 December 1920, Dick Kerr Ladies played St Helens Ladies at Goodison Park, home of Everton, before a crowd of 53,000 and raised over £3,000 for charity. During 1921, they played 67 games all over the country, watched by a total of 900,000 people.

By this time women's teams were everywhere, not just their games being reported in the papers and their teams captured on postcards but also in cartoons, illustrations and in fiction. Many comics began running stories of women's teams, such as the weekly magazine *The Football and Sports Favourite*. In 1922 they featured 'Nell O'Newcastle – a thrilling story of a girl's footer team', which ran for weeks and weeks.

Cartoonists and illustrators also had a great time, some portraying women playing football in a rather glamorous light, such as the girl in the so-called Bachelor Girl's Club. My card was

posted on 29 August 1905, so the postmark says, and so does a date on the front written in ink. The date confirms what had been happening in ladies football since Miss Honeyball and her gels ten years earlier – knickerbockers had been getting shorter and shirts more like the male version and a lot shapelier, though no doubt the artist had used a bit of licence when drawing the bust line.

One of the First World War's most eminent illustrators, Fred Spurgin (1882–1968), better known for his patriotic cards, produced a series of humorous cards with a lot of saucy play on words showing women playing football. 'A fine all-round player' has, of course, an excellent figure. Judging by the even shorter shorts and the way the boots are tied, I guess these cards must have come out around the 1920s. Some experts, such as the National Football Museum, have dated them as 1890s, which is unlikely from the football strips and also the fact that Spurgin was born in 1882 and was far too young to have done them.

In each of the cards, the games taking place involve women playing with men, which did happen as mixed teams became popular in the 1920s – done for charity and fun and probably a few high jinks.

And then on 5 December 1921, the rotten old FA banned women's football. They did it indirectly, but wickedly, not banning the playing of the game by women – for how could they do that? – but banning any male club that was a member of the FA from letting women players use their ground.

There were two main objections. One was on health and medical grounds, backed up by many doctors who said that football was bad for women, they were not strong enough, their bodies were not made for it and they would never bear children. The fact that for four long years they had been doing really heavy manual work in munitions factories, and survived, doesn't seem to have been taken into account. The other objection was more of a smear, suggesting that some sort of fiddle was going on, that money from the large gates was not in fact all going to charity – as if the men's game from the very beginning had not been full of financial fiddles, gate receipts disappearing and underhand payments.

The FA ban did not put an end to women playing football, or its popularity. Women's teams played on rugby grounds and in parks, and all through the '20s and '30s, girls' footer stories still appeared in magazines and women players appeared regularly in *Punch* cartoons and elsewhere. Comic cards continued to feature them, right up to and after the Second World War, usually of the seaside variety, with busty players being asked if they wanted to swap shirts.

Dick Kerr Ladies carried on playing, though they renamed themselves Preston Ladies in the 1930s, raising thousands for charity and going on more foreign tours, including to the USA and Canada. They finally packed up in 1965 – thus missing the massive revival of women's football we see around the world today.

Chapter Eight

THE GREAT UNKNOWNS

When did footballers start having their photographs taken like footballers have their photographs taken? It has now become a tribal thing, copied by teams all over the world. Once a photographer appears, they group themselves into neat lines of either two or three rows. In that hasty shot before kick-off, the smaller players will go down on their haunches at the front, arms folded, while the bigger lads will stand at the back. For the formal shot, say at the training ground at the beginning of the season, a bench of sorts will be brought out and they will arrange themselves in three rows – one row on the ground, one on the bench, and the other standing at the back. When it comes to a mass picture featuring the whole squad, which these days can outnumber the population of Botswana, especially if it includes trainers and coaching staff, they still try to organise themselves into three rows – as nature intended.

They do it because that's how it's done, how they have seen it done when they were growing up, so posterity will know you were a proper football team. They know without being told that you should fold your arms and keep your legs slightly apart if you are on the front row.

Burglars really do say, when apprehended on the job, 'It's a fair cop,' because that's what they believe burglars say. Footballers do say they feel as sick as a parrot or over the moon or gutted, because that's what other footballers before them have said.

In those very early Harrow and other public school photographs, back in the days before leagues and professionalism, the players didn't arrange themselves in formal, serried ranks. The front row might be sitting down, for obvious reasons, so that others behind who are standing can be seen, but otherwise they felt free to take up their own individual poses, looking languid, looking bored, hand on head, hand on chin, looking away. They are superior people and not going to be bossed around by any jumped-up photographer johnny trying to regiment them for his own purposes or following any popular fashion.

My theory is that the strictly arranged three rows, with all players striking the same pose, came in for two reasons. Firstly, they were aping the formation on the field. Once proper programmes were printed, which, of course, did not happen with the early public school games, players took up the formation as it appeared in the programmes, which often included little illustrations. For almost 100 years, a football team's formation was the same everywhere. There were five forwards – outside left, inside left, centre-forward, inside right, outside right – three in the middle – left half, centre half, right half – and three at the back – left back, goalie, right back.

This is how it was till at least the 1960s, as you can see in all football programmes, where the players are still listed in three lines, with five forwards at the front, even if by then they were not always playing in that exact formation.

In the classic photograph of any team from 1890s onwards, that was the basic set-up. In most photographs five normally sat at the front, who were usually the smaller players, three in the middle row and three at the back with the goalie in the centre. This arrangement would be altered slightly if the team had won some trophy and it was being displayed, in which case the captain might sit in the front row in the middle, holding the trophy or, if not that, the ball. Sometimes it would be only two rows, but all the same the forwards tended to be at the front and the defenders at the back, with the goalie in the middle, as they were on the park and in the programme.

It was the postcard photographers who arrived in their thousands from 1900 onwards who formalised something that had happened naturally. They wanted to make a team look like a team, however amateur and modest, in the correct formation, and they requested arms folded, look this way, don't smile. The team itself wanted to look as smart and team-like as possible. They were going to send these cards to their family and loved ones, so they hoped to look their best and most impressive.

The vast majority of football postcards, of which millions were produced between 1900 and 1939, were of Unknown Teams. The smallest, most humble, most local, most useless team would always aim to get itself photographed once a year, just as the real professional teams did, and have postcards made.

You can generally tell a professional team because they don't write anything on the ball. They know who they are and what they have won. However, in printing the postcard of a professional team, the manufacturers will usually add the name of the team, the season and often the team line-up in a printed caption underneath or on the back.

With amateur teams you rarely, alas, get the team named and the players identified – hence they have become the Great Unknowns. The most you get is the year painted in white on the ball, which fades and becomes hard to read, plus now and again the initials of the team. Decades later it is impossible to work out what 'LPSC Football Team' stands for, what 'EBA FC' means, where 'Regent' came from, or when it says Rovers or Rangers, which Rovers or Rangers did they refer to. You have to hope for a clue on the back giving the photographer's address or a scribbled message or postmark.

They all knew who they were, who everyone else was and what they had done, so there seemed at the time no need to identify themselves. These cards were for private consumption, to be posted or given to friends, not sold to strangers on stalls around the country. A hundred or so years later, these teams have mostly vanished, the players have disappeared from sight and from memory, lost and forgotten – but not by me.

I see my Unknown Footballers like Unknown Soldiers, representing all the millions who came before and who came afterwards. I can stare into their faces for hours, wondering what became of them – did they survive the First World War, did they become unemployed, join the Jarrow marchers, emigrate abroad, join up again in the Second War?

At the time, they were either looking back at the season just finished or just about to begin, remembering great games, great events, great enjoyment. Professional players, once they retire, are always harking back to the dressing-room, about the crack, the tricks, the jokes, the laughs, the camaraderie and how they now miss it. The Great Unknowns also had their happy times, seasons to remember and reasons to rejoice, things they never forgot. I study them and think, now, was he the joker, the moaner, the wide boy, the lady's man, the dum dum, the butt of all the jokes?

I started off buying these Unknown Teams because they were cheap compared with famous teams, which have grown more and more expensive over the years. I stuck them all in one album at first, but when I got to about one hundred, I had to get another album. When I got to 300, I began to see a different pattern. As with the professional teams, I could see changes and developments, like boots and shirts, or if the ball had an end patch, but I could also see the different social communities they represented. Or so I imagined.

I then found myself arranging them under different categories, for my own amusement, with different headings, putting them in different albums. Excellent therapy when I was recovering from a knee replacement.

EARLY UNKNOWNS

Even though the teams are unnamed and undated, I began to look out for teams that must be pretty old, from around the 1900s, or the 1890s if I could find any, trying to identify the period by looking out for anyone wearing belts or long shorts and whether the goalie had the same style shirt as everyone else.

TRADITIONAL THREE ROWS

These are teams that had arranged themselves perfectly in what I like to think is the traditional format – five at the front, three in the middle, three at the back. Some are smart, erect, arms folded, and some not quite so regimented, some sitting on the ground, some on chairs, but all still 5-3-3s.

Early unknowns, sitting in the traditional three rows of 5–3–3.
The ball says 'Coronation 1900–1', so was that their name?
You can tell it was early by the belts and the ball's shape.

ROUGHLY THREE ROWS

With these, I imagine that they set out to be 5-3-3, but things got a bit disorganised, with someone mucking up the pattern by deciding to stand at the back, or they wanted to shove a notice or pot at the front in a prominent place. In the case of a team called LPSC, they have only two at the front – one of them a goalie. Now that is unusual. Was he an unusually small goalie?

STUDIO SHOTS

Most postcards show the team on the pitch, before or after a game, but now and again the team did what most ordinary people did before everyone had cameras – they trooped along to the local studio. You can tell the studio shots, if you look carefully, by the drapes in the background, a carpet on the floor and by the fact that all their strips are immaculate and their hair is ever so neatly combed and brushed, as if their mother had done it for them.

POSH TEAMS

If there are cloisters in the background, or an imposing portico, the chances are it is a public school or some sort of good college team. Often the trainers/masters are very well dressed, in blazers, with scarves round their neck, perhaps an academic gown or even someone in evening dress. The material of their strips usually looks of better quality than normal, with rather fancy badges.

Above: Traditional three rows: a church team, perhaps, and early, going by the ball.

Middle: Still 5–3–3, if not quite straight: 1913 Wednesday Interleague, printed in Reading.

Below: Three rows, but 2–5–4. Who was LPSC? 1915–16.

WORKERS' TEAMS

It's only a guess, and they could well be the Eton 6th XI, but when some are in what look like their normal working clothes and boots and appear as if they have just come off the night shift, this does suggest they are some sort of factory team. Someone in uniform at the side, like a postman or railwayman, is also a clue. They still try to look smart and proud, arranging themselves into a proper line-up, but the fact that they have different-coloured socks and shorts does rather suggest they have had to buy their own kit.

ODD STRIPS

On the other hand, odd strips could suggest a rather bohemian, arty lot who could afford proper gear but preferred to be casual, showing they are a Sunday-morning, coats-for-goalposts, who's-picking-the-sides-this-week team, the sort I used to play with for many years, who turn up for fun, putting on whatever strip comes to hand or just playing skins against the rest. Simply having a knockabout in the park doesn't often lead to a postcard, but I have one taken at Rock Park, Barnstaple – possibly schoolboys during their break.

SMART STRIPS

I mean this not only in the sense of being in perfectly matching strips but also in interesting, quality designs with nice stripes or pretty Vs. Sweet.

Above: Smart strips, unusual line–up and a studio shot, judging by the carpet, 1911–12.

Middle: Three rows, studio shot, but which Rovers? 1910–11.

Below: Possibly posh, or could be a college team. 1912–13.

BIG WINNERS

It amuses me to see teams who have won loads, who have trophies and cups bigger than some of the players, who are desperate to let the world see how well they have done. So sad that it is now almost impossible to know what it was they won their pots for.

MESSAGES

As most of the postcards of Unknown Teams were sent to loved ones, they very often identified themselves by adding arrows, or giving the names of all the players, or perhaps the score, plus a message, which is always helpful.

Above right: Big winners, Spensley AFC, 1912–13 – but of what?

Above left: Bring on the workers. Have they just come off a shift?

Middle: Odd strips, perhaps a dads' team, after a kickabout.

Below: Smart strips, if a rather odd line-up.

MILITARY

This is a vast category, as military officers as well as the public schools played an important part in the beginnings of football. The top army teams always did well in the FA Cup until the professionals came along. All regiments and units had their own teams, and naturally they got their photographs taken each season. You can't tell if they are military from their strip – only if someone in some sort of military uniform is standing at the side.

UNUSUAL LINE-UPS

These are the teams who break the mould, and they have always existed, who refuse to pose in that boring traditional formation and instead decide to stand in one straight line across the goalmouth for their team picture – which

Above left: St John's College, plus message – but where? Posted in 1905.

Above right: Military divisional–cup winners, 1917–18.

Middle: Military, but with female supporters. No date or place.

Below: Odd line–up. Pity the poor photographer.

must have made it hellishly difficult for the photographer, trying to get them all in the shot. Then there are the clever clogs determined to create new and unusual formations, with players lying on the ground at different angles, facing different ways, making pretty patterns – or so they think.

YOUTH TEAMS

They got their photos taken as well, in the school or young club, or junior team, just as they do today, and some of them are incredibly smart. If they are in a playground, you can assume it is a school team and that the school paid for the strip, but when they are sitting in a field, or out in the country, you wonder who paid for all their kit. Adoring mums, presumably.

MASCOTS

Mascots today mean two things – those silly figures in animal costumes who jump around at the side of the pitch and sweet little boys and girls who accompany the team out. Mascots in the second sense have long appeared in team photos, usually sitting at the front, looking cute. No doubt they were the child of one of the players, the captain or manager, or they might have been the ball boy. Sometimes, or so it would appear, a dog was the mascot – unless, of course, he'd just walked into the shot.

Above: Blessed youth: sitting ever so nicely, and in three traditional rows, different strips, but nice caps. No date, but 1900s by the look of the ball. Fine Art Studios, Bradford.

Middle: Even younger youths, equally old postcard, but no clues.

Below: Mascot: the little boy at the front is either that, a ball boy or the son of a player.

Single: in the back garden, legs crossed, hands together, now shoot . . .

Trios: two with great belts, in the back yard, yet the photographer is F.W. Spry, Littlehampton. Perhaps he came to the house.

SINGLES, DOUBLES AND TRIOS

Many players would appear to have been so proud of their team and their strip, and fancied themselves in it, that they trooped to the local studio on their own and sat there, posing, then sent copies to people, letting them see what a hell of a feller. Others stood with one or two of their chums in the back garden, looking a bit sheepish.

BLACK PLAYERS

In the one thousand cards I have of Unknown UK Teams up to the 1950s, I have yet to come across a black team – in fact, I have only come across one team with a black player. He sits at the side of a large team group in what looks like some institution, perhaps a college. They are all wearing badges on their shirts, but I can't make them out. On the back, someone has written 'Portsmouth?' in pencil, so that could be a clue.

And yet in professional football, black players had existed from the beginning, though there were very, very few, rarely more than one or two in

Black player lurking on the far right. Looks like some sort of college.

Unusual cards: Fancy dress, charity game? Photographer is F.C Sharpe, Hitchin.

each generation. Arthur Wharton joined Preston North End as an amateur in 1886 and signed as a professional with Rotherham in 1889. Even before that, in the wholly amateur days, Andrew Watson played for Queen's Park in 1874. Walter Tull played for Spurs in 1909, then Northampton Town. He was an officer in the First World War – said to be the first ever black officer – and was killed at the Somme. Black players then almost totally disappeared from League football until the 1960s, so I suppose in a way the postcards were only reflecting society as a whole.

UNUSUAL CARDS

Roughly, this means cards of Unknown Teams and players I have not been able to fit into other sections. They include a football team with a giant ball, 1900s by the look of their strip, possibly for some charity event; a more modern card with players dressed as women, presumably for some student rag event; a school team with no ball and no strip, mostly in blazers; and a team photo that has more players in suits – 20 – than in strips – 13.

I also include a traditional line-up, 5-3-3, with a fancy decorated border, which must have made a very nice card to send to friends.

KNOWN UNKNOWNS

When I am studying these teams, I often wonder if any of them became famous, went on perhaps to be millionaires, artists, politicians, or went to prison.

I do have two cards where I can identify a face. One is of my dad in 1935, playing for an RAF team somewhere in Scotland, where he was stationed at the time. The other is also Scottish, a club called Fetlor who were an Edinburgh boys' club supported by two of Edinburgh's well-known public schools, Fettes and Loretto. In the second-back row of their 1949 line, you can see someone who later became a well-known thespian: Sean Connery. He was a good player, played semi-professional and later, while touring with the cast of *South Pacific* in Manchester, Matt Busby saw him play for a show business team and offered him a trial with Man United – but he never took it.

Known unknowns. RAF team in Scotland, 1935.
My dear dad, John Davies, is in the back row, third from right.

Fetlor, Edinburgh, 1949. Second back row, second right: Sean Connery.

I am still one day hoping to find a postcard of the University of Algiers team in the 1930s showing Albert Camus in goal. 'All that I know most surely about morality and obligations of man, I owe to football,' so he later wrote. How true.

Vladimir Nabokov was also a goalie while studying at Trinity College, Cambridge, in 1919. Surely someone somewhere has a postcard of him in his college team. Do keep an eye out.

I do have one card of a really scruffy, horrible-looking team from the 1980s called Dartmouth Park United. The title does make them sound like a proper team, and we did register with the Greater London Council in order to book a proper pitch each Sunday morning on Hampstead Heath – but it was indeed a scruffy, scrappy team made up of local dads and we wore any old thing.

We picked two teams each week, depending on how many turned up.

I played with them for ten years, such happy times, what fun, oh I wish I was playing now. I did continue till I was almost fifty, which was really stupid, despite having two cartilage ops. I got to the stage when I felt fit enough to play football – but not fit enough to recover from playing football.

One season we got our photie took and made cards, so posterity would know what we all looked like. Two of those dads did go on to become well-known people, life peers, in fact – Melvyn Bragg (now Lord Bragg) and Bernard Donoughue (now Lord Donoughue). They are both in the back row – Bernard is second from left and Melvyn fourth from right. I am in the front, fourth from left, and still unhonoured. Bastards.

Now knowns: Dartmouth Park United, 1980. I am on the front row, fourth from left, still a commoner, while in the back row are Lord Bragg, fourth from right, and Lord Donoughue, second from left.

Chapter Nine

SONNY'S PLAYTIME

A good "Kick off". Yes, that's the sort
Of thing that helps the game to win:
But there's a kick that isn't sport,
And that's a kick that barks the shin.
Yet, shin or not, it's all the same;
A British boy will "play the game".

FOOTBALL.

Talk not of war's alarms;
Football hath greater charms;
Better than feats of arms,
Are feats of feet.
Let then your guns be mute;
Call only those who shoot
Goals with unerring boot/
Heroes complete.

GREETINGS

You can tell that something has passed into everyday life when references or images of it appear on everyday-life things.

In stage one, football's appeal was to those interested in football, hence you have postcards of teams, football programmes and football magazines catering directly and specifically to football fans. Then it moved out, entered the language and seeped into our general social and economic life. One of the earliest signs of football's popularity and acceptance was its use in greetings cards. Football was used as an image, with references and words that everyone would understand even if they didn't play or watch or know anything about football.

Christmas cards were quick on the scene, for Christmas-card manufacturers have always

I wish you a Christmas full of fun.

Late Victorian greetings card, possibly 1890s, judging by the ball and cap, when already society had generally accepted that football was full of fun.

Christmas card, 1890s, with ribbon, raised image of a ball through a window
and some really corny verse using football phrases.

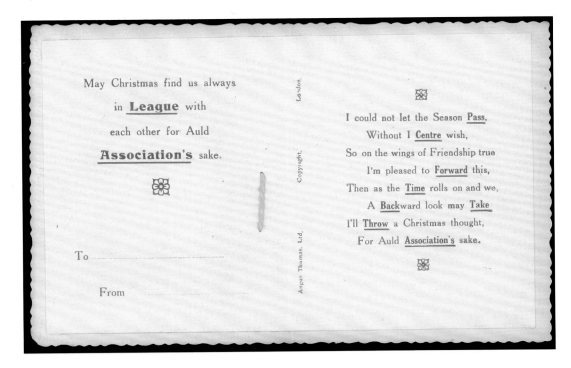

May Christmas find us always

in **League** with

each other for Auld

Association's sake.

To

From

London.

Copyright.

Angus Thomas. Ltd.

I could not let the Season **Pass**,

Without I **Centre** wish,

So on the wings of Friendship true

I'm pleased to **Forward** this,

Then as the **Time** rolls on and we,

A **Backward** look may **Take**

I'll **Throw** a Christmas thought,

For Auld **Association's** sake.

been looking for new angles and new themes instead of snow and holly and all that stuff. The first known Christmas card was sent by Sir Henry Cole in 1843. He didn't have time to send personal Christmas greetings to all his friends that year so asked a printer, John Callcott Horsley, to design and print some festive-looking cards. The ones left over of the one thousand printed were sold by the printer at one shilling each, which was very expensive, so he must have done well.

The card showed a happy family enjoying a festive glass – which was condemned by anti-alcohol campaigners for encouraging drunkenness. They didn't catch on at first, perhaps for this reason, not really till the 1860s, but then in the 1880s they became incredibly popular and all Christmas-card manufacturers were looking for new angles and different presentation.

'I wish you a Christmas full of fun' says the message on one early Christmas card – and what was the idea of fun that Christmas? Football, of course. I'm not sure which year it was, but judging by the shape of the ball and the fact that the player is wearing a cap, it must be late Victorian, perhaps 1890s.

Christmas cards were being sent – inside envelopes – long before picture postcards, thanks to all the Royal Mail regulations, so it's pretty likely that football Christmas cards, meaning those with a football image, were around well before we had proper football postcards.

Christmas cards of the 1890s became very fancy, with embroidery, raised decorations, ribbons and bits stuck on, which must have been complicated to print, but labour was cheap in those days. The one with the ball stuck on looks quite plain when reproduced, but in reality it is three-dimensional, with a stuck-on ribbed ball seen through a window. Inside, the Christmas message is full of football references. The ball has a patch, which makes it Victorian, and the use of the word 'association' hints at the same period, as by around 1900 the word 'football' was generally used without the need to use the full term, 'Association Football'. But of course the word

Also 1890s, also with awful puns on a football phrase, but cleverly printed with three – dimensional pads and shirts, though you can't tell in this photo.

'association' was being used in this Christmas context to suggest old friends.

The Christmas card with the two players kicking the ball is also three-dimensional, with the players slightly raised. They appear to be wearing shin guards over their socks, and long shorts, which indicate the card's age. Note also the corny puns about football – 'un-toe-ward incident' – which, of course, never age.

Along with Christmas cards, birthday football cards were very popular, some photographic with yucky little twee verses – still going strong. But you don't see many New Year almanac cards today, such as the one overleaf for 1908, giving you a calendar for the year ahead, plus a cartoon.

Two birthday cards, probably 1930s, using a football:
left, a Rotary photo, London, and right, W&K Cards.

Almanack card for 1908, with football image, produced by Millar and Lang, Glasgow.

TO MY VALENTINE

A FOOTBALL ENTHUSIAST
YOU SHOUT ALL DAY ON SATURDAY,
AND COME HOME BLACK AND BLUE;
ALL SPLASHED WITH MUD FROM HEAD TO FOOT—
I'LL NEVER MARRY YOU.

Valentine's card, presumably meant to
be funny, but pretty savage.

GUSSIE: "Oh, no, I nevah play football; I think the costume makes a fellah look so widiculous, y'know."

An anti-football card, but ironic.

Lots of birthday cards featured football, as did valentine cards. I hadn't realised that the idea of abusive valentines was so old, the sort very popular today, though of course they are meant to be funny and not to be taken personally. The one showing a loudmouthed, huge mouthed footballer who shouts all day on Saturday and comes home filthy looks suspiciously serious, as if the girl sending it was really not going to marry him if he carries on with his footer.

Once football got going, there were often anti-footer cards showing the perils of football, how scary and rough it could be, especially if you were a little kid in goals or being kicked around. Then of course there were those who criticised football for its loutish overtones and bad behaviour – and also its unattractive, unflattering clothes. In one caricature of a gent saying that football

costume is 'widiculous', he of course looks pretty ridiculous himself.

But in the main, greetings cards used football to convey a happy, amusing or uplifting message, which of course the Victorians loved, using any means to emphasise all the right virtues, which was what the public schools were doing when they encouraged football in the first place. 'A British boy will play the game,' says one card, while another suggests that playing football will get you ready for the really rough games in life. In one, though, there is a distinctly pacifist message, advocating that guns should be mute – 'Talk not of war's alarms, football hath greater charms, better than feats of arms, are feats of feet' – which is a message FIFA would like to think it is sending out to the world today. That card was posted in Newcastle on 5 February, but I can't read the year. Could it

A good "Kick off". Yes, that's the sort
  Of thing that helps the game to win:
But there's a kick that isn't sport,
  And that's a kick that barks the shin.
Yet, shin or not, it's all the same;
  A British boy will "play the game".

No clue to artist or date,
but printed in Saxony.

FOOTBALL.
Talk not of war's alarms,
Football hath greater charms;
Better than feats of arms,
  Are feats of feet.
Let then your guns be mute;
Call only those who shoot
Goals with unerring boot,
  Heroes complete.

Valentine's Series.

Some of the verses carried serious messages, moral or patriotic or pacifist.

A rather nice stylised watercolour, no publisher names.

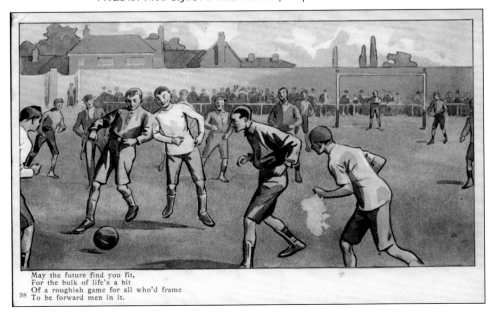

May the future find you fit,
For the bulk of life's a bit
Of a roughish game for all who'd frame
98 To be forward men in it.

THE HOPE OF HIS SIDE !!

·BOTTLED·UP·

JACK BROADRICK.

Two anti-footer cards, showing the rougher side of football for the weedy and titchy.

A soppy and a wholesome card.

The final.

Still dribbling along.

HIS FIRST "FOOTER"

I MUST'NT BE LATE FOR THE "KICK-OFF."

The Hope of His Side.

P. 20.

THE KICK OFF.

Opposite page: More soppy cards. Published by (clockwise from above left) Regent, London; E.H. Atkinson; Hart, London; and Coronation, London.

Above left: 'The Kick Off' was printed commercially in Saxony and posted from New Zealand in 1912, which indicates how international football had become.

Above right: The baby appears to be a real baby, not a model, done privately for family and friends.

Right: The boy holding an old–fashioned ball also looks real – possibly Victorian.

FORWARD! GREETINGS!

A greetings card so awful, so badly done, in such awful colours, that one hopes it was done in Saxony as well. But no details.

have been wartime? Surely not during the First World War. Perhaps it was just afterwards.

Amongst the most popular greetings postcards with a football theme were the straightforward illustrations of sweet little children. Some were full-colour artwork, usually fairly soppy drawings with soppy captions, such as 'Still dribbling along.'

There were also many Real Photographs, commercially produced by normal postcard manufacturers, as you can tell by their name on the back and a printed caption underneath the photograph. 'His First Footer,' says a little boy holding a ball. In another, a baby with a ball is saying, 'I mustn't be late for the kick-off.' This one was addressed to Master Willie Eadis in Glasgow and the message in pencil reads, 'Dear Willie, I wish I was beside you to give you a big hug and a lot of kisses for your birthday.'

I like it when messages on postcards are written in pencil, as so many were, as of course there were no biros in those days, because they can be rubbed out and used again. I have done that for years, recycling old cards and sending them to my own loved ones on their birthdays or Christmas – and are they grateful, are they amused? Are they heckers. I don't know why I bother.

Thousands and thousands of personal greetings cards were done by people for themselves – Real Photographs of their little darlings, to send to friends and relatives. Like those Unknown Teams, these now Unknown People trooped along to a studio to get little Willie or Harry or Isa or May photographed in their best clothes holding a football, or had them done at home, in their back garden. Because the children loved football? Even that baby, too young to toddle, far less kick a ball? Possibly. But the point is that football was acceptable, recognisable, healthy, popular, part of national life.

Chapter Ten

Find the Referee.

After the Match was over.

what an ass-
-pect

COMIC FOOTBALL CARDS

You have to laugh, being a football fan, or else it's tears, screams and shouts, kicking the wall, kicking the cat.

I often think it must have been quite nice being a football fan between the years 1863 and 1888. There were no leagues, no falling to the bottom of the table, no hated rivals being above you, no ups and downs, no dreaded drops, no going right to the wire, for there was no wire. You constantly played friendlies. Oh, life must have been so calm and pleasant then, so little aggravation, so little pain and disappointment.

Apart, of course, from the Cup. Once that began in 1872, Cup games became huge, the most important part of the season, and once you were knocked out, especially if you considered you were a top club, that was it, your season was over, you might as well give up, go away and lock yourself in a darkened room until next season. It was like dying, being knocked out of the Cup.

And that was the big joke, of course. Some of the earliest and wittiest and most artistic of football comic cards were not the obvious lurid, garishly coloured comic cards but the rather subtle, neatly designed cards known as In Memoriam cards.

The concept was that the team that was knocked out was now deceased, hence a funeral was being held in its memory, so a card with a black border and some suitable verse got printed to mark this sad and touching occasion. Real *in memoriam* cards, and envelopes and writing paper, all with a black border, announcing the death of a loved one were at one time common amongst all classes, so the joke was readily understood, but today they have disappeared.

These football versions of *in memoriam* cards were often sold at the ground, immediately after the Cup match, which was very clever. Certain smart manufacturers, in order to get ahead of their rivals and not lose sales, would even print in advance two different cards – mourning the defeat of both teams, just in case.

The 'In Memory of Manchester City' card of 1910 was for a real piece of giant killing. On 5

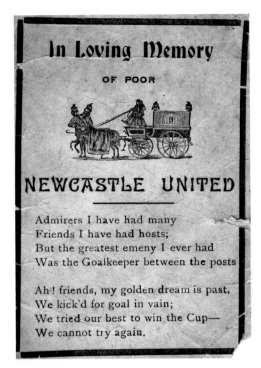

In Loving Memory of

NOTTS. COUNTY

O'er the Magpie's Tomb, with silent grief oppressed,
Notts. supporters mourn their hero's now at rest,
And their vain hopes have now passed'away,
And bid farewell to the cup until some future day.

In Loving Memory

OF POOR

NEWCASTLE UNITED

Admirers I have had many
Friends I have had hosts;
But the greatest emeny I ever had
Was the Goalkeeper between the posts

Ah! friends, my golden dream is past,
We kick'd for goal in vain;
We tried our best to win the Cup—
We cannot try again.

In Memoriam cards, mocking the defeated teams in a cup match, 1900s. The image of a funeral cortège and coach appeared in many of them. They were done locally and often printed in advance in two versions: mourning each team, just in case.

March that year, the season in which Man City won the Second Division Championship and got promoted to the First, they were beaten 2–0 in the fourth round of the Cup at the County Ground, Swindon. Swindon at the time were non-League and didn't make the Football League, Third Division, till 1920. What a turn-up. I'm sure they still talk about it in Swindon. The note at the end, 'Funeral arrangements by GWR', refers of course to the Great Western Railway, on whose trains the poor old Man City fans would have been trundling home.

One month earlier, the same card, with the same artwork of a funeral coach at the top and the same typography, was issued – but with a different verse to celebrate a different event. This time it had been when Swindon had beaten Spurs in the second round. It was produced by the same local printer, Maybury's of Swindon. They clearly enjoyed having a dig at the big-time charlies from London and mocking their defeat – 'Toll the Bell for the Spurs that Fell'.

Such cards were produced in towns all over the country for big cup games, knowing there were going to be big crowds and big sales, even if many of their cards had to be dumped once the event was over.

It's interesting that the same image of a funeral stagecoach was used in relation to a team called Fusiliers, presumably an army team, but the wording is less precise. It doesn't say who beat them, or where or when. The card is very well printed, but the word 'Fusiliers' is a bit rough, as if it had been stamped in on the day, perhaps after the game, with some sort of John Bull Printing device. Doing it that way, they could keep a supply of basic football In Memoriam cards to be used after any Cup game as the occasion demanded.

In Memoriam cards for specific games and big teams are today pretty expensive as few have survived, having a short shelf life and being limited to one locality. (I paid one hundred pounds for that Man City one at Sotheby's in October 2009, but don't let on.)

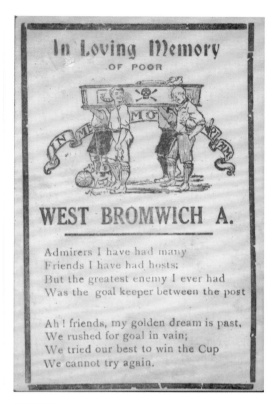

In Loving Memory

OF POOR

WEST BROMWICH A.

Admirers I have had many
Friends I have had hosts;
But the greatest enemy I ever had
Was the goal keeper between the post

Ah! friends, my golden dream is past,
We rushed for goal in vain;
We tried our best to win the Cup
We cannot try again.

IN MEMORY OF
Manchester
CITY.
WHO FELL AT
The County Ground, Swindon
FIGHTING FOR THE
ENGLISH CUP.
MARCH 5TH, 1910.
AGED 4TH, ROUND.

Bury Manchester City
Their day is over and done,
Sing them a little sad ditty
And cheer for the team that won,
Oh don't you think 'twas rather a pity
You came to Swindon, Manchester City

Funeral arrangements by G.W.R.

Now and again, cards were produced to sympathise with the losing team, rather than rubbishing them, though they are very rare and I still haven't got one, but Eric Krieger quotes one in his book *Good Old Soccer*:

> Boldly to the fray we went
> On honour fame and vict'ry bent
> But with sad hearts we came away
> For the match we'd lost today
> Our opponents they were far too good
> In fact we stood like logs of wood
> Our chance is past, our day is o'er
> At football we will play no more
> RIP

Coloured cartoon cards on general football themes were the most common comic cards of all and were on sale everywhere to all football fans. They often came in sets so you could collect them as well as send them, illustrating a series of football phrases, such as a goal or a foul, half-time or transfer. It was the drawing that was meant to be funny more than the caption, which was limited to a few words.

Weedy, puny players were often mocked for being scared when confronted by hulking defenders – 'Go on little un, push him orf it!' – and were shown in bandages after it was all over. Brains versus Beef is still a common theme, at least in British football. It was a dirty, muddy game as well as rough, so a masher – which is what a smooth, trendy man about town was called in the 1900s – would expect a hard time.

There were a lot of military cards produced and posted during the First World War showing soldiers playing in their encampments. I used to believe it might all just be a legend – the stories

Above: The West Brom card, sympathising rather than rejoicing, was probably produced locally in Birmingham.

Below: The Swindon card, gloating in victory over Man City in 1910, was produced in Swindon by Maybury's.

A FOU(W)L?

HALF-TIME.

WE SHALL MISS THE PATTER OF YOUR LITTLE FEET

of troops playing while in the trenches and how they once played against the Germans on Christmas Eve, before they went back to killing each other. We now know that incident was true, as documentary evidence, in the form of a soldier's diary, has recently revealed.

Referees, of course, were fair game for mockery, although perhaps not in the very early days, when they knew their place, which was on the touchline, and knew their role, which was to shout or wave a flag. Once he was given a whistle and controlled the game from the middle, there was a flood of music-hall and cartoon jokes about referees losing their whistle. One of them was by Donald McGill, more usually associated with other sorts of comic cards.

There were a great many comic-card artists, working full-time and producing hundreds of different cards every year. One of the best known in his day was Tom Browne. He was born in Nottingham in 1870 and served his apprenticeship as a printer before starting to produce sketches and cartoons in his spare time. He came to London in 1895 and got some freelance work with the postcard manufacturers and also for various comic papers, his best-known comic characters being Weary Willie and Tired Tim. He began the London Sketch Club with some fellow artists, as he saw himself as an artist, not just a hack illustrator and cartoonist. His artwork, with very bold lines and vivid colour, was much admired. He contributed to *Punch*, exhibited at the Royal Academy and became a member of the Royal Society of British Artists. He died of throat cancer in 1910, aged only 39. Today his work is highly collectible, though perhaps not as expensive or as popular as McGill's.

Footer puns, of a sort.

Above and middle: Published by Millar and Lang, Glasgow. No artist named.

Below: Printed in Holland, posted to Bath in 1913.

Palatine Limerick card, one of a series. A 'masher' was a smart chap about town.

The word 'transfer' had passed into the language by 1905. Published by Jackson, Grimsby.

Brains v. Beef, a common theme in comic cards.

Posted in Truro, Nova Scotia, Canada, 1908.

Posted in Richmond, Surrey, 1912.

Soldiers did play football at the front in the First World War. This card, by the Photochrom Co. of London and Tunbridge Wells, was posted from Keswick to Carlisle on 14 June 1915. Middle and below: Referees were fair game for unfair comments, right from the moment they got their first whistle, in 1878. In 1893, the Referees' Association was formed.

Drawn by Donald McGill, posted in 1913 in Kentish Town, London, written in French to an address in Allier.

Posted 1915. Another gem by Millar and Lang of Glasgow.

More fun poked at the refs.

Left and middle: By Tom Browne, one of the best-known comic-card artists. Note that his joke about the ref swallowing his whistle was also used by Donald McGill and probably scores of others.

No artist named, but produced by the National Series, posted 12 March 1905 in Sydenham, South London, to a Mr Pat Murphy. The message on the back says, 'Dear Pat, hope it won't happen like on the 25th of March. If so your head will be out of order instead of your knee.'

"BEG PARDON. MY MISTAKE." "FOOTBALL."

"FOOTBALL."

STIFF CHARGE.

Donald McGill, today the best known of all the comic-card artists, was born of Scottish descent in London in 1875. When he was 16, he lost a foot while playing rugby and was fitted with an artificial limb. He trained as an engineering draughtsman and was almost thirty before he moved into drawing picture postcards, starting at six shillings a time. He went on to draw thousands but was never all that well paid. It was the postcard manufacturers who made all the money.

During the First World War, McGill did lots of military cards showing weary Tommies and also loads of sentimental, soppy ones featuring children and dogs. In one of them, a dog is pulling at a little girl's dress while she is praying beside her bed. 'Please Lord excuse me a minute,' reads the caption 'while I kick Fido.' He reworked that postcard, the words and the drawing, and in all it sold three and a half million copies.

But he was best known for his saucy seaside postcards, many of them showing fat, big-bosomed women and weedy men, drunks, honeymoon couples, vicars, and innocent young girls and older, lusty men making suggestive comments that the young girl does not quite get. Most of them depend on double entendres.

Two women are hanging out their washing. 'Your night dress is looking rather the worse for wear,' says one. 'Well dear, it's seen some ups and down in its time,' replies the other.

'Did the doctor find out what was wrong with you?' asks a mother to her attractive and rather glowing daughter. 'Oh yes – he put his finger on the spot at once.'

'Do you keep stationery?' asks a man in a bookshop to a pretty assistant. 'Well I wriggle sometimes,' she replies.

Three cards by Tom Browne, 1900, produced by Davidson Bros, London and New York. On the back it says, 'From Originals by Tom Browne, R.I', indicating that he was seen as a proper artist, not just a postcard hack. He contributed to *Punch* and was a member of the Royal Society of British Artists.

'THINK YOUR HUSBAND'S GOT A LONG ONE – KEEPS TRIPPING OVER HIS!'

'Do you like Kipling?' says a man to a pretty young girl. 'I don't know, you naughty boy, I've never been kipled.' That card was said to be his most popular and sold six million copies.

During McGill's long career, his saucier postcards were continually being attacked by local watch committees, who were keepers of the nation's morals, saying such postcards were corrupting our children and young people. He had his high-class defenders, such as George Orwell, who wrote an article in 1941 in the magazine *Horizon* describing McGill's work as folk art and praised it as it blew 'a chorus of raspberries' at prissy authorities. It didn't, however, save McGill from the dreaded watch committee, and in 1954, aged 80, he was prosecuted in Lincoln for alleged obscenity. His craven publishers persuaded him to plead guilty and he was fined £50. He died in 1962 aged 87.

He didn't do a huge number of football-related postcards, but the few he did were of the saucy variety, such as a young boy looking at a theatre poster that shows a big-breasted woman. 'That reminds me – I must blow out my football when

Some saucier football postcards.

Above: Produced by Cardtoon series in 1970.

Right: By Donald McGill, posted 1955. The joke has rather dated: no one blows up footballs today, though busts may be.

I get home.' Today, that joke would have to be reworked – now that footballs don't get blown up and breasts could well be silicone implants.

There were hundreds of other comic artists who used football as a theme for their saucy seaside postcards, knowing football fans were the sort who went to the seaside and liked their sauce.

Suggesting swapping shirts with lady players probably first originated back in 1895 in Crouch End, when the British Ladies first played, but it continued as a hardy annual for decades and is still going strong today.

The drunken Wembley joke, about someone mistaking Wembley for Wednesday, was so popular it was pinched by many postcard manufacturers and also appeared on beer mats. Jokes about knickers also have a long, har har, history.

Of the cleaner football jokes sold at the seaside, the one about the teacher and the pupil

"That reminds me – I must blow out my football when I get home!"

"IS THIS WEMBLEY?" "NO, IT'S THURSDAY."
"SO AM I. LET'S GO AND SATISFY OUR BEER BUDS."

Some safer jokes. Above left: Various versions of the 'Wembley drunks' jokes appeared on lots of different cards and also on beer mats. Above right: One of the National Series, posted 1914. Bottom right: All it says on the back is H.B. Ltd London EC1, not posted, no message, but it looks 1930s. The joke still works, though a modern version would probably substitute 'Fust an' Second Division' for Premiership.

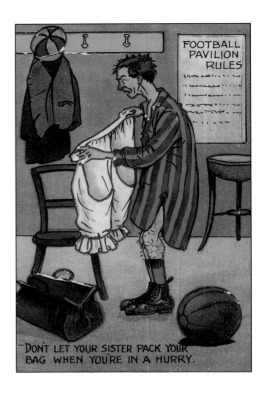

DON'T LET YOUR SISTER PACK YOUR BAG WHEN YOU'RE IN A HURRY.

"WHO BEAT THE PHILISTINES?"
"DUNNO, SIR – I ONLY FOLLER THE TEAMS IN THE FUST AN' SECOND DIVISION!"

could still be used today, although the reference to the Second Division might be changed to the Championship.

'Who beat the Philistines?'

'Dunno sir – I only foller the teams in the First and Second divisions.'

But it was the saucy ones that sold best – and I have to admit they are ones I enjoy. The one about the Lady Mayoress coming into the dressing-room to autograph the players' balls is a bit obvious – but it does represent a truth about dressing-rooms.

When I was writing a book about Spurs in 1972, I spent a lot of time in their dressing-room. There was always a large pile of balls waiting to be autographed on a table in the middle of the dressing-room. They were mainly for charity, of course, and each player, as he arrived for training or a game, would dutifully add his own signature to each ball.

Slightly ruder cards. Above by Bamforth and below by Sapphire, but both convey football truths. Players still sign footballs in the dressing room for charity. Touts, though rare, can be seen now and again. Alas, brass bands playing live at half-time, walking round the pitch, are no more.

About 25 years later, I was again at the Spurs training ground. By chance I opened the wrong door, thinking it was the manager's, and stepped into a room where a secretary was sitting. At her feet she had a large supply of pristine white balls and in front of her, propped up on her desk, was a large photostat of the autographs of each player in the first-team pool. She quickly put her arms over her desk, but it was obvious what she was doing – and understandable. Modern players are just too damn busy to sign their own signatures.

I think my favourite comic footer card, though, is the one showing the tout selling tickets for ten pounds.

'£10 for a ticket!' exclaims a fan. 'I can get a woman for that.'

'Yes!' replies the tout. 'But not 45 minutes each way and a brass band at half-time!'

Obviously I do not approve of such sexist jokes, which demean women, but I am interested in them for historical reasons, oh yes.

Only ten pounds for a ticket, – that is a period piece for a start. And the reference to a brass band at half-time. For almost a century, brass bands were a feature of all professional games. The local band, from the Sally Army to the police to the town band, marched out at half-time and paraded round the pitch, in full uniform, with their band leader twirling his baton and the crowd holding its breath, hoping he would drop it so they could all laugh and jeer.

At Arsenal for many years they had a really excellent metropolitan police band who played semi-classical and light musical hits. I can still see them now, crouching on the far touch-line, watching the game for free, of course, waiting for their moment at half-time to stride out and do their bit.

I particularly enjoyed the archaic wording they always used in the Arsenal programme. I have one in front of me, from the Arsenal–Carlisle United programme of 6 January 1951. (I wasn't there, but sat listening to the wireless back at home in Carlisle, hoping that our lads under manager Bill Shankly would stuff those stuck-up cockneys. In fact we did good, getting a draw – then got hammered in the replay at Brunton Park, which I did attend.)

According to the programme that day, the police band played excerpts from *Coppélia* by Léo Delibes, the 'Overture' for *Rosamunde* by Schubert and a selection from *King's Rhapsody* by Ivor Novello. Oh, all quality tunes. Under

Find the Referee.

what an ass—
—pect

Produced by Woolstone Bros, the Milton series,
posted 1903 to Towcester. Someone has written
their own joke on front: 'What an ass—pect.'

After the Match was over.

Another well—worn joke from
Millar and Lang, Glasgow.

that day's list of music the following words were always printed: 'All engagements are by permission of the Commissioner of the Police of the Metropolis, Sir Harold Scott, KCB, KBE, and subject to the exigencies of the service.' It was the word 'exigencies' I loved. Don't think I have ever seen it in a football programme since.

Generations of fans brought up on watching and listening to live brass-band music at League games must long for the good old days. Instead they have to suffer all this boring too loud music at half-time or rubbish commercials on the big screen.

Touts standing outside grounds, holding up tickets for the game, were also an enormous presence at all big games till the last decade or

so. I used to rely on them at one time, when I went to Arsenal, as I wasn't a season-ticket holder there. I used to wait till the last minute, when they were desperate, and if you only wanted one ticket, anywhere, you would always get one relatively cheap. My rule of thumb was never to pay more than 50 per cent above the cover price. Usually it was more like 20 per cent – which you can pay today buying any sort of desirable ticket online.

Touts served a purpose. People arriving with a spare ticket, because someone had not turned up, could always sell it to a tout. I remember being surprised when I recognised some touts standing outside White Hart Lane – and realised they were the same people who the previous Saturday had been standing outside Highbury. It was clear that

the same families had been working as North London football touts for generations.

Today, touts outside the ground have all but disappeared at football matches. Perhaps some survive on the Net, selling them on eBay, but they can't do the business they did in the old days, as almost all tickets are season tickets, sold by the year, one season ahead. Tickets for individual games are dying out. Soon we'll just have a flash card or digital thingy or DNA recognition to let us in.

Turnstiles – they will disappear as well. Already at some grounds, such as the Emirates, you just need a slot to slide your card into. When I went to Portugal for the Euros in 2006, all the grounds were like that. Those massive ironwork turnstiles will soon be obsolete. In my mind, I can still hear them creaking, then having to squeeze through while a grumpy old man in a muffler tears up your ticket and you eventually shoot through at the end, released from captivity into the pleasure dome.

You can defend saucy cards by saying they were surreptitiously subverting the moral codes and attitudes of the day, mocking the pompous, deflating the prudes, airing the thoughts and feelings of ordinary people that would otherwise not be mentioned in polite circles. On the other hand, by playing on certain prejudices and stereotypes they were endorsing rather than sending up sexist attitudes with their verbal winks and pictorial nudge nudges.

Any road up, saucy cards may be saucy to some, reprehensible to others, but to me they are all social history.

Tom Browne's version of a popular football pun.

A FULL BACK.

Portrait of the Referee after the Match.

F.B. "A SUCCESSION OF CORNER-KICKS
PROVED INEFFECTUAL."

The sort of kick I hope
you will never be called
upon to administer.

Above left: More fun poked at a poor old ref. Above right: Tut, tut, not the sort of corner
kick we want to see. Below: Tom Browne again with more puns.

HEAD
WORK.

Chapter Eleven

LANGUAGE

When football entered our life, it brought with it new words, new phrases and, in fact, almost a new language, which eventually went around the whole world.

There were technical phrases, or at least existing words that took on new meanings when applied to football, such as 'goal', 'penalty' and 'foul', which then passed into general usage with the football meaning attached, but were also still used on everyday non-football occasions. 'Moving the goalposts', for example, is used by businessmen everywhere, usually when they are complaining. They start business meetings by saying 'let's kick off' as if they are at a football game. 'A level playing field' is what they all aim for, unless, of course, they are the ones who have secured all the Big Players. 'Playing in a different league' or 'we are now playing in the big league' were surely not normal expressions till the football leagues were created.

The use of the phrase 'political football' was heard in Parliament from the nineteenth century to describe a subject that gets kicked around, battered and bashed, and very often ends up 'kicked into touch'.

A 'hat-trick' now refers to three of anything but is still used in football to mean the same player scoring three goals in the same game and thus claiming the match ball – if he can find it. There are now so many. Actually, a hat-trick is supposed to have originated in cricket, when it meant a bowler taking three wickets in three bowls, but we'll ignore that as the term was given general currency from the 1870s onwards, thanks to entering football speak.

'Back to square one' is believed to have originated in the 1930s, when the BBC first started broadcasting live games on the radio. To help listeners follow what was going on, the *Radio Times* printed a plan of a football pitch marked out in eight boxes, each one numbered. One commentator described the play while another said which square they were now in – which always ended with going back to square one, with a goalkick.

A FINE FULL BACK, AND A GOOD CENTRE FORWARD.

By Fred Spurgin, posted 1921, produced by A&H Footer series – standing for Art and Humour. A play on the words 'Centre Forward' – meaning someone with a big belly – appeared on hordes of cards. In the 1920s, when women's football was very popular, a 'Full Back' was a way of suggesting, 'Does my bum look big in this?'

Politicians particularly enjoy using current phrases from football to show they are modern and in touch, but the other day on the radio I was surprised to hear the newly appointed Archbishop of Westminster, the Most Rev. Vincent Nichols, come out with a football cliché. He was congratulated on his new job and replied, 'I will give it my best shot.' In *The Guardian*, I read a political story in which someone 'took an early bath at a G20 meeting'. Then in *The Independent*, Dominic Lawson criticised political spin doctors in an article called 'Playing the man and not the ball'.

Posted 1915 in Dover to Canterbury, this card has a message which reads, 'Dear Mother, just a line to see if you are still alive as it is ages since I heard from you. With love from all, Lizzie.'

"CENTRE FORWARD"
(Very much so).

After all these decades, football is still coining new similes and metaphors, which get picked up by people from all walks of life.

Football postcards made a feature of football phrases early doors, by which I mean from around at least 1900 onwards, and they remained a running theme in a great many comic cards from then on – with the same jokes being repeated every generation, with only the drawings brought up to date.

They fall roughly into two types. First of all there are visual jokes – a play on words used in football, illustrating them with another meaning, such as a centre-forward is a fat person with his centre, that is his belly, well to the fore, which must be about the hoariest ever football joke. Fortunately, with the advent of strikers, the use of the word centre-forward is becoming less used, so the joke could be on its last legs, or relegated to the bench.

I have a set of cards called the Herriot series, produced by William Collins in Glasgow, which were entitled Football Phrases Illustrated, showing a corner, a throw-in and so on, and, inevitably, a centre-forward. The postmark is 1904, so perhaps they were about the first to use that joke. If so, well done. After that, centre-forward jokes were used all the time. In the 1920s, when women's football was very popular, the topical angle was to include a hefty female full-back – gerrit – along with the tubby male centre-forward.

Three of a set of cards, posted between 1904 and 1906, nicely designed with little drawings of players round the side, entitled Football Phrases Illustrated, produced by William Collins, Glasgow. It took the words and phrases of football, which by now had moved into the language generally, and illustrated them in non-football situations.

Women, once they started playing regularly, were often described as fast players – meaning they were sexually flirtatious – though the use of the word 'fast' as applied to a woman is not quite as common as it once was. They are all fast today, so I am led to believe.

Sexist football cards made a lot of play on the word 'transfer', suggesting that blokes would like to transfer their wives. 'Transfer Talk' was a running headline in most newspapers once Alf Common went to Boro in 1905. 'A bargain at £10,000' says a caption on one card, which suggests the 1920s, when the first £10,000 transfer took place.

There were also lots of harmless twee cards using football puns, usually showing very young children with captions like 'His First Match', 'The Little Dribbler' and 'Just Signed On'.

A Bamforth card from 1960 managed to get three football phrases into one joke. It shows a little

Just signed on.

Football puns. Above left: Bamforth,1920s, using the term 'transfer' to suggest a transfer from the wife. Above right: Corny pun on Aristophot card, posted 1909.

Bamforth, 1960, manages three footer phrases.

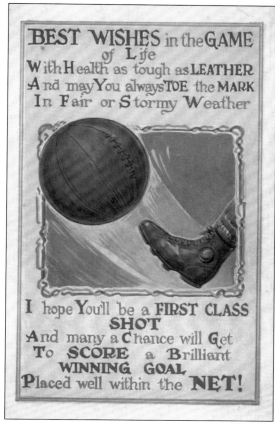

BEST WISHES in the GAME
of Life
With Health as tough as LEATHER
And may You always TOE the MARK
In Fair or Stormy Weather

I hope You'll be a FIRST CLASS
SHOT
And many a Chance will Get
To SCORE a Brilliant
WINNING GOAL
Placed well within the NET!

Left: Greetings card, 1920s, with football words.
'Leather' was another name for a ball.

Below: The football pools, which began in 1923,
introduced new words into the football lexicon,
such as 'dividend' and 'nothing barred'. A blotter
card from Littlewoods, which you could post or
use to blot your inky entries.

such as 'great dividends' and 'nothing barred', phrases that were understood by everyone who filled in their pools coupon each week.

Once the Football League began in 1888, there were suddenly exciting, important games to watch every Saturday afternoon, with results to speculate about. Newspapers cashed in on this interest by offering prizes for those who could

weedy husband and his big wife, who is hogging the whole bed. 'I shall have to whistle you offside again Agnes – why the heck can't you stay in your own half!' The year 1960 is written inside the cartoon, but the use of the name Agnes makes it sound as if it was originally drawn much earlier.

As well as all the visual gags, there were many that relied mainly on verbal puns, using football words and phrases in verses to wish people a happy Christmas or good luck generally.

> Best wishes in the GAME of Life.
> With Health as tough as LEATHER.
> And may You always TOE the MARK,
> In Fair and Stormy Weather.

The football pools, which grew out of football, provided another set of words and phrases that could be used in postcards and greetings cards,

WHO IS HE?

HE'S ONE OF THE PENNIES THAT WON A BIG DIVIDEND ON LITTLEWOODS!

BLOTTER
USE WITH YOUR COUPON

A Christmas card aimed at pools players and stuffed with loads of football phrases, two per line, which must have been a winning combination that scored heavily with the punters.

A LEAGUE OF HAPPINESS POINTS TO A DIVISION OF JOY IN ALL FIXTURES AT THIS SEASON. HOPING YOU KICK OFF IN GOOD FORM AND WILL BE IN THE CENTRE OF A COMBINATION OF FUN AND FROLIC, PASS FORWARD TO THE NEW YEAR RIGHT WELL, AND BACK GOOD LUCK IN EVERY QUARTER, WIN NEW FRIENDS, AND DRAW FROM THE CUP OF PROSPERITY TO THE FULL. ALL BEST WISHES TO YOU

1X2 HOME OR AWAY 21X

2X2 1

COPYRIGHT

Christmas Greetings
And
ALL BEST WISHES FOR YOU
HAPPINESS IN THE NEW YEAR

From ....

guess the result of certain games. It started in 1888 at about one pound for a correct answer, then went up every season when papers realised how popular it was and how it increased sales and got them publicity. By 1911, a magazine called *The Umpire* was offering three hundred pounds for readers who correctly predicted the results of six fixtures.

Bookmakers, who traditionally had stuck to horse racing, then piled in, offering their own odds. In 1923, the first known independent football pools appeared, with coupons issued separately from any newspaper by a Birmingham bookmaking firm called Frederick Jarvis. Other firms quickly followed. They had a lot of trouble with the betting laws and various regulations, but in the 1930s football-pools companies were doing enormous business. By 1939, £800,000 a week was being collected by the leading pools companies, notably Littlewoods and Vernons, both based in Liverpool.

In 1948, when normal football life and leagues had resumed after the war, the pools were doing even better – taking in fifty million pounds a year from eight million punters. And the government was making a fortune from them in a pools tax.

I remember as a boy in the 1950s having to fill in and then check my father's pools for him, as he was an invalid. He did the Treble Chance, whereby, as far as I can remember, you marked the results of the game with an X, a 2 or a 1 – meaning a draw, an away win or a home win. A draw got you three points. Each week, there was a huge Treble Chance win, up to £100,000 in 1950, along with thousands of smaller winners each week who got a tenner. I don't remember us winning anything. Not a sausage, which is what my dad used to say every week at ten past five after we had listened to the results on Sports Report.

The pools was part of everyday life, and most families took part, asking each other on Mondays at work if their coupons had come up, how many points did they have and was there a dividend. The pools people issued their own cards – in one example from Littlewoods, it also doubled up as a blotter for, of course, people used fountain pens, not biros.

Some of the pools-related cards were much more elaborate than ordinary cards. They were often nicely coloured, with attractive lettering, which opened to reveal a message inside, repeating the football theme. On one, which has a player heading the ball, it says 'Headed for Yuletide's Pool of Happiness'.

On the backs of all football postcards, if they have a handwritten message, I always look out for football words and phrases in use at the time by footballers, football reporters and football fans, some of which have now become obsolete. A ball at one time would be referred to as the Bladder or the Sphere or the Leather. A goalkeeper was a Custodian of the Nets, or just Custodian. Knickers were, of course, shorts.

I look out for words generally to see the changes and fashions in ordinary language. People wrote their cards in a more colloquial, everyday language than the more formal style used for writing a letter, when people sat down properly, sucked their lip, poised their pen and tried to compose correctly as opposed to dashing off a quick message.

Pre the First World War, favourite words and phrases to indicate that something was good included the word 'topping' along with 'ripping', 'capital', 'champion', 'top hole' and 'spiffing'. 'Capital' and 'champion' were particularly common when describing footballers – a capital half-back, a champion centre-forward.

After the Great War, came 'super', 'marvellous', 'A1', 'stupendous', 'excellent', 'fabulous' and 'riveting'.

After the Second World War and into so-called modern times, terms of praise have included 'smashing', 'stunning', 'terrific', 'fab', 'awesome', 'brill' and 'wicked'.

All these words were usually accompanied by adjectives and adverbs stressing just how spiffing or super things really were, words that also came in and out of fashion – such as 'jolly', 'awfully', 'absolutely', 'utterly', 'amazingly', 'pretty', 'dead', 'bloody', 'pretty bloody', 'dead bloody good' or 'f***ing bloody awful', which alas can be found written on some postcards today by uncouth supporters with no sense of taste or style or history.

An even more elaborate pools Christmas card, with puns. The writer excelled him—
or herself with football words that slipped easily into normal language.

AROUND THIS **SEASON** MAY PLENTY OF **FIXTURES** PROVIDE YOU WITH A **LEAGUE** OF HAPPY TIMES AND A **TEAM** OF FRIENDSHIP. HOPING YOU **KICK OFF** WITH PLENTY OF FUN IN THE **CENTRE** OF FESTIVITIES, WITH A GOOD **RESERVE** OF HEALTH AND HAPPINESS TO **PASS** YOU WITH ALL JOY, WELL **FORWARD** INTO THE NEW YEAR, AND **FORM** A NEW KNOT IN THE **TIE** OF OLD FRIENDSHIP

COPYRIGHT

Remembrances and the Best of Good Wishes for Christmas - - - and the New Year.

From *Mother — La Nellie*

Chapter Twelve

TRADE AND COMMERCE

I s anything ever new? Hardly ever completely new, certainly not in football. Every time we have a World Cup or big footer event, the newsagents shops are filled with new and shiny little packets of football cards or stickers and kids in playgrounds all over the country, and the globe for that matter, go mad spending all their pocket money on them, trying to collect whatever it is that they are currently being urged to collect.

These trade cards were and are essentially little postcards showing a player or a team, not postcards in the posting sense, although there have been periods when they have been postable, but they were and are collected and treasured like postcards.

The term trade card can be a bit confusing. In the world of collecting, it can refer to two types of cards. Both have their own meaning in the wonderful world of football memorabilia.

First, a trade card is a card or a sticker that you have to buy in packets, which then get traded, little boys or girls swapping them amongst themselves, trading them for ones they want or haven't got.

Baines cards were the original version of football stickers, begun by John Baines in Bradford in 1887. You collected six in a packet for a halfpenny.

Baines cards came in different shapes, such as hearts and shields, and were beautifully coloured. Mostly they carried exhortations like 'Play Up' and 'Hurrah', followed by the team's name, but they could also commiserate or mock the referee.

On the reverse side, Baines boasted about their awards, that they were the sole inventors and to beware feeble imitations.

£100 A YEAR GIVEN IN PRIZES.
Buy BAINES' ½d. Packet of
Cricket and Football Cards
By Royal Letters Patent, No. 80607.
Sold by all respectable Tobacconists, Stationers,
and Confectioners.
The Largest Football Card Printer in the World.
Estimates given for any quantity.

J. BAINES, Sole Inventor and Patentee of the
½d. Packet of Cricket and Football Cards,
65, Carlisle Road, Manningham, and
15, North Parade, Bradford.

N.B.—Boys buy these Cards for collecting
purposes. They are sought after
as eagerly as ancient stamps.

Baines, having started in Bradford, went national and by 1920 were producing 13.5 million cards a year: the largest football-card printer in the world.

Late Victorian playing cards, a football version of Happy Families, representing all the family.
The father is how I looked after every game.

Second, it refers to cards produced by trading companies – commercial companies who make things like sweets and bubble gum or newspapers or magazines – which make football cards in order to promote and sell their products, usually giving them away for free if you buy the product or subscribe to the magazine.

Trade cards, meaning cards that kids bought and traded, came first and were invented in 1887 by John Baines of Bradford. He was at one time a tobacconist and a toy maker in Bradford, till he hit on the idea of selling packets of football cards to his little customers. Baines cards, as they were always known, even when rival manufacturers copied them, were the first mass-market product to cash in on the popularity of football. They are also, in my opinion, still the most beautiful and artistic souvenir football items ever manufactured. It was not surprising that Sir Peter Blake RA, the eminent artist, used them in a screen print he produced in the 1970s called *F for Football*.

Today, examples of Baines cards in good condition fetch up to forty pounds each, though you can get examples in tatty condition for half that price, which tend to be the ones I have, but even then you can admire the colouring, the artwork, the design and the football illustration in the middle. They are quite small, usually three inches by two, but such care has been taken with them compared with the cheap, nasty, ill-printed trade and sticker cards that appear today.

They came in different shapes – a shield, heart, diamond or circle – showing club colours, players or a football scene, with a slogan and usually the name of the club. The slogans were exhortations on the lines of 'Play Up Oldham' or 'Now's Your Chance, Manchester' or congratulations like 'Well Dribbled Everton' or 'Cardiff Takes the Cake'.

You got six different cards in a packet for a halfpenny – randomly selected in that you didn't know which ones you had till you opened the packet. Now and again, if you were lucky, you found a special card that was termed a Master card or Gold card, which was very rare. You collected them, swapping doubles with friends, trying to get as many as possible.

There were prizes you could send off for if you had completed a set or had a Master card. The prizes were usually football equipment. Such objects were greatly desired, as the ordinary boy in 1900 could not afford proper boots or even a ball. As late as the 1950s, I remember the status someone in the playground had if he actually owned his own leather football. Everybody wanted to be his friend.

Baines cards started off at first featuring local Yorkshire clubs, then the north-east, then they covered the whole country, on sale everywhere. On the backs, it said they were made by J. Baines, 'the sole inventor and patentee of the ½d packet of Football Cards'. And to make their point even clearer, it sometimes added, 'Do not be gulled by worthless and feeble imitations.'

Soon they were boasting on the back 'By Royal Letters Patent' and 'Gold Medal Football Cards', meaning they had won awards at Trades Exhibitions. Then they were adding advertisements on the back for products such as Pears soap. Clearly Mr Baines was a smart operator.

There is a contemporary account of a man in Bradford watching little boys peering through the windows of the printer where Baines cards were produced, gazing longingly at them being turned out in their thousands. It was clever to have a printing works with a window on the street, so prospective buyers could ogle the goods.

Mr Baines himself died in 1908, but his son took over the firm and they were going strong till the 1920s. In 1920 alone, some 13.5 million Baines cards were produced and sold. I am indebted for this figure to Alexander Jackson, who is currently working on a PhD at Leeds Metropolitan University and has done a research project on Baines cards – see, I told you how classy they are. He also told me, which I didn't know, that adults also used to collect Baines cards and stick them in their coat lapels or their hat bands when going to games, showing which team they favoured. I must get a really good magnifying glass and look at those old crowd scenes again.

Having said that Baines cards were the first to commercially exploit football, I was thinking of

Silks: made of silky cotton, 1920s, produced by BDV Cigarettes, showing a player from your favourite team in his colours.

the mass market and in that particular way. There were, of course, many products around from the same period that occasionally featured a football motif or image, like toys and biscuit tins.

I have a rather precious set of Victorian playing cards – precious because I paid a lot for them, though I can't remember now quite how much. I had to compete with collectors of playing cards, not just football cards, which put the price up. They are a football form of Happy Families, probably from the 1890s to 1900, judging by the shin guards over the socks. The illustrations are very colourful and attractive and amusing, showing a Mother and Daughter each playing football, while the Grandmother doesn't appear to be playing – she just gets hit by a ball. The Father, who has a moustache, is wearing bandages and carrying a crutch after being injured in a game. He does remind me of somebody – me. That's how I looked every Sunday till I was 50, when at last I gave up.

One very early and unusual form of football 'card' that has not been repeated, as far as I am aware, or adapted to modern use, unlike the Baines cards, were what are known today as Silks. They were postcard-sized or larger pieces of a silk-like material – some form of fine cotton by the feel of them – on which were printed a coloured

image of a footballer. They were produced by a cigarette company called BDV and either given away in packets of their cigarettes or perhaps you sent away for them, as a special offer, when you had collected enough ordinary cards or answered certain questions. They are very classy and even in 1922, when they appeared, must have been fairly expensive to produce. Even now, after all these decades, the ones I have are still in great condition, with the colours hardly faded. Printing in colour on actual fabric was part of the selling point because they featured football shirts. They came in a series called League Colours so you could collect the strips of all the famous teams. I assume the image was somehow transferred onto the material, so it's now a piece of textile history as well as of football.

I wonder if fans, once they collected their favourite teams, sewed the silks onto their own clothes, to wear when going to a match, or on their pyjamas. That way they could support their fave team, sporting their colours, even while fast asleep.

The other main type of football trade cards – the ones produced by firms and magazines to promote goods and sales – tended to be photographic, not artwork, and mostly they did look like ordinary postcards, though some were bigger, some smaller.

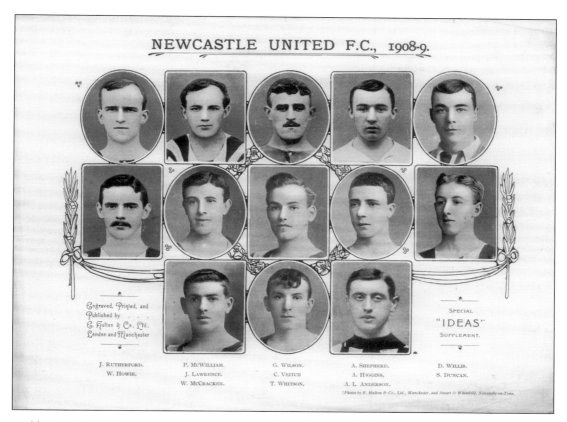

NEWCASTLE UNITED F.C., 1908-9.

Engraved, Printed, and
Published by
E. Hulton & Co. Ltd.
London and Manchester.

SPECIAL
"IDEAS"
SUPPLEMENT.

J. RUTHERFORD.   P. McWILLIAM.   G. WILSON.   A. SHEPHERD.   D. WILLIS.

W. HOWIE.   J. LAWRENCE.   C. VEITCH.   A. HIGGINS.   S. DUNCAN.

W. McCRACKEN.   T. WHITSON.   A. L. ANDERSON.

[Photo by E. Hulton & Co., Ltd., Manchester, and Stuart & Whitfield, Newcastle-on-Tyne.

Many magazines, newspapers and comics offered free football cards as circulation boosters.
Newcastle United, 1908–09, came with *Ideas*.

They were also more informative, usually with lots of details, facts and figures on the back. Much as I love Baines cards and the Silks, they are little works of art rather than a reliable source of football information.

In 1908, the excellent magazine *Ideas* gave away a large-format card of the current Newcastle United team. It's very well printed and designed and each player is clearly seen – and named, which is always a great help. *Ideas* ran for many decades and was a large-format general weekly magazine that covered 'Fiction, Fact and Fancy', so it said on the masthead. It usually had a full-colour illustration on the cover, often with a football theme, and some of the latest football news inside. Let's hope that doing a football supplement, and giving away such a nice photograph, did prove a sales booster.

A magazine called *Gee's Weekly* produced some cards showing football scenes, like taking a penalty kick, which were well drawn and coloured.

The magazines, comics and newspapers that catered primarily for either boys or football fans, such as *Boys Magazine* and *Topical Times*, gave away football cards in almost every issue all the year round in order to keep up their sales.

In our house, despite living in Carlisle, we listened to the Scottish Home Service and read the Scottish newspapers. I still have a *Scottish Daily Express* Super Sports Postcard showing the Scottish team, in civvies, before the Scotland–England game at Hampden on 14 April 1956. Rather poor card and badly printed, but they were all my heroes.

TAKING A PENALTY KICK (1).

published by "GEE'S WEEKLY.

On the back, it boasts about next week's issue of the paper. 'What a week ahead for NEWS. The Russian Visit! The Budget and THAT Wedding. As ever, the *Scottish Daily Express* is the paper for the BIG OCCASION.' You can't accuse football fans of not knowing what was going on in the rest of the world, though I have to admit I can't remember which Russian was visiting or who was getting married.

Sweet and biscuit companies also issued sets of football postcards as promotional gifts. Typhoo Tea, not a product you would associate directly with small boys, did some very well-produced full-colour team cards.

Ardath Cigarettes in the 1930s did a long-running series of photocards – much bigger than cigarette cards. My set goes up to No. 109, but

Left: *Gee's Weekly*, 1920s, offered a good-quality postcard with a pretty bit of artwork on how to take a penalty.

Below: The *Scottish Daily Express* in 1956 gave away a rather flimsy black-and-white card of the Scotland team – but they were all my heroes (result: 1–1).

No. 11—Scottish Daily Express Super Sports Postcards.

Front Row—Glen, McMillan and Docherty (reserve). Second row—Hewie, Parker, Reilly, Leggat. Third row—Smith, Johnstone, Younger and trainer Dowdells. At the back—Young (captain) and Evans.

Scotland v. England—Hampden Park, April 14, 1956.

ABERDEEN F.C.

Another thin cheapo card, part of an extensive series on famous English and Scottish teams given away by Shermans Pools, Cardiff, 1938–9.

there were probably hundreds more. Apart from giants like Heart of Midlothian and Bradford City, who for some reason are all wearing goalies' jerseys, it includes some teams I have never heard of, such as Grove House FC, who played in the West End Business House Intermediate League, and the Gaumont Picture Corps FC who had recently won the Kinematography Cup. I assume they covered every team in the English and Scottish leagues, and when they ran out of them, featured any old club they could get photographs of. They do list all the names, and the clubs honours, so are invaluable.

Shermans Pools did a rather flimsy set called 'Shermans Searchlight on Famous Teams', but at least they had a direct connection with football. *Hotspur*, my favourite comic, was still issuing postcards of famous teams in the 1950s, complete with histories of each one. The magazine *Sport* did a very glossy series of teams in full colour, which came in a little album.

One of the tricks that Mr Baines missed was to encourage boys to collect their cards and then stick them in albums – special albums printed with pockets or pages into which you could stick your cards. You had to write away for these albums and often had to pay extra. Hence this development on the Baines cards later on became known as stickers.

All collectors today now look upon this as a hanging offence, pure sacrilege – imagine being so stupid as to stick your precious cards in an album, thus ruining the card and totally obliterating whatever was on the back. You will find, when you go round the fairs, that the price of completed pre-war albums is surprisingly low, whether of cigarette cards or postcards, if they happen to be all stuck in, yet 80 years ago they must have brought tears of joy to the boy or girl who had completed this feat, who had collected the whole set and also got the album. Now dealers treat such completed albums almost with

TOTTENHAM HOTSPUR F.C. 1949-50.
Back row, left to right. W. Nicholson. A. Ramsey. H. Clarke. E. Ditchburn. R. Burgess. L. Medley.
Front row, left to right. C. Withers. W. Walters. W. Rees. L. Duquemin. E. Baily.
PRESENTED BY SPORT.

BURY F.C. 1949-50.
Back row, left to right. H. Whitworth. W. Griffiths. D. Clegg. L. Bardsley. G. Griffiths. C. Fairclough.
Front row, left to right. G. Hazlett. F. Worthington. D. Massart. H. Bodle. W. Barclay.
PRESENTED BY SPORT.

Above: In 1949–50, the magazine *Sport* offered glossy colour postcards – well, you can see the green of the grass – of famous teams in little stapled booklets.

Above right: The awful records produced by the England and Scotland teams in recent years were not quite new. In the 1890s, you could buy the sheet music of something called the 'National Football Song'.

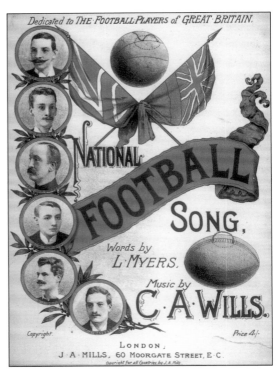

contempt. A set of 25 individual cards not stuck in will fetch twice as much as a set stuck in, even in its special album. So it goes. That's collecting for you.

Cards as an advertising vehicle are fairly thin on the ground, at least in the UK. Baines put adverts on the back of his cards, but I am really thinking of a football card used as an advertising medium in itself. Shermans Pools were in a way doing that, issuing football cards with their name on, but mainstream manufacturers not connected with football rarely seemed to have used football postcards to promote their wares. They did it a great deal in newspaper and magazine advertisements – for Oxo, Sloan's Liniment and Ellimans Rub, which all players were said to use to increase their health, fitness and scoring ability. Oxo did produce a few football cards as a vehicle for itself, such as the 1904 Cup final when they had both the final teams praising the wonders of Oxo, but there were not many. Perhaps the size of a postcard did not really lend itself to advertising.

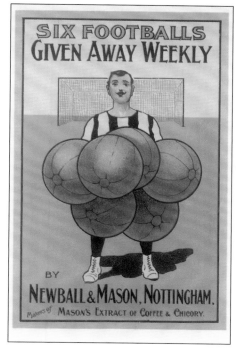

Railways, 1923, and coffee makers, 1890s, used football to sell their stuff.

Hull Co-Op Stores in 1936 did one better and got actual footballers to promote their clothing.
Let's hope the lads all got a free suit.

YOU CAN'T PICK A TEAM TO SUIT EVERYBODY, BUT—
HULL CO-OPERATIVE SOCIETY'S CLOTHING IS ALWAYS SELECTED BY GOOD JUDGES OF STYLE & FORM.
WHO'S WHO IN HULL CITY—
19 Yorke. 20 Quantick. 21 Annables. 22 Pearson. 23 Maddison. 24 Tabram 25 Simpson. 26 Dimbleby.
Mr. Menzies (Sec.-Manager), 18 Llewellyn, 17 Don, 16 Foster, 15 Woodhead, 14 Denby, 13 Edwards, 12 Gray, 11 J. Lodge (Assist.-Trainer), 10 J. Beck (Trainer)
1 Baldry. 2 Mayson. 3 Hubbard. 4 Acquroff. 5 Holmes. 6 Spivey. 7 Bell. 8 Davies. 9 Cassidy.

SUNDERLAND F.C. 1949-50.
Back row, left to right. B. Johnston (Trainer) J. Stelling, A. Hudgell, J. Mapson, W. Watson, W. Walsh, T. McLain, A. Wright.
Front row, left to right. T. Wright, I. Broadis, R. Davis, Mr. W. Murray (Manager) L. Shackleton, T. Reynolds.
PRESENTED BY SPORT.

SOUTHPORT F.C. 1949-50.
Back row, left to right. J. Street, C. Beardshaw, T. Hitchen, W. Birkett, W. Bellas, R. Hacking, H. Boyle, G. Mutch (Trainer)
Front row, left to right. E. Rothwell, A. Dainty, F. Walsh, C. Wyles, R. Maddison.
PRESENTED BY SPORT.

Two more freebies presented by *Sport* magazine. The colours of Sunderland can at least be seen clearly. Note Len Shackleton, second right in the front row. He wrote his autobiography in 1955, in which the chapter headed 'The Average Director's Knowledge of Football' was left totally blank.

There were lots of football songs at one time, in the 1900s to 1920s, a lot of them featuring poor old referees. In order to sell the sheet music, postcards were produced, such as one featuring something called 'The National Football Song'.

There were cards issued by football-equipment manufacturers, such as Newball and Mason in Nottingham, which count as football cards, as they show a football theme, as well as those issued by big stores such as Gamages, which sold a huge amount of football gear. Railway companies, when they were laying on special trains for the Cup final, did postcards with a football theme.

Now and again local shops and firms managed to persuade their local team to appear on postcards, promoting their wares. Bolton Wanderers were used by a Bolton cigar shop, Shepherd. The promotion was for El Honor cigars, which were said to 'score every time'.

I am rather fond of one piece of blatant advertising that the players of Hull City agreed to in the 1930s. They appeared on a postcard issued by the Hull Co-operative store, each of them sitting holding up a number to identify himself – which makes them appear like judges at a talent show. Most of them seem amused, others a bit embarrassed. The caption states that 'Hull Co-operative Society's Clothing is always selected by Good Judges of Style and Form'. I hope they got a decent fee, or perhaps a cheap half-decent suit.

Chapter Thirteen

FOOTBALL INCIDENTS.
OXFORD v. CAMBRIDGE (Association).

ART, FASHION, POLITICS

The very earliest football postcards were little works of art for the simple reason that there were no half-decent photographs of football games available. The main postcard manufacturers, such as Raphael Tuck, the biggest and most famous of them all, commissioned real-life artists to draw imagined scenes or incidents from football games. From 1902 onwards, Tuck produced postcards that they called Oilettes, which became the generic title for lots of similar coloured postcards. It would appear that the drawing was done first of all in black and white by the artist, then coloured in by the Tuck studios. Presumably some sort of oil-based paint was used, as they do seem richer than watercolours or crayons.

With thousands of competing postcard manufacturers, national and local, they were always boasting about their latest special, exclusive, state-of-the-art methods, especially at the top

Pop into A&G Taylor of Sunderland and South Shields in the 1900s and you could capture yourself in 'Platinotype, Bromide and Carbon'.

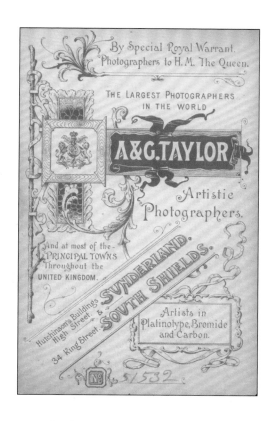

A Raphael Tuck Oilette showing a football scene. Created by S.T. Dadd, a proper artist, hence his credit line. Posted in 1907 in Harleston, Norfolk.

Some of the competitors in the Oilette field were not as artistic as Mr Dadd. In one card I have, the player's head seems drawn on by a different artist or had perhaps been copied, if not very well, from a photograph. It is a Tuck card, so it says on the back, but a Tuck's Postkarte, so perhaps it was a foreign team, painted abroad, hence that striped strip I don't recognise.

I have three nicely drawn and coloured cards I consider very artistic. One is very old and shows a player with a moustache taking a kick at a ball. The other is of a goalie in a cap and red jersey, which was originally a poster, painted by J. Petts in the 1930s, and reproduced as a postcard by the National Football Museum. The third figure is a player in white with the ball at his feet against a plain blue background (again done

Another of Dadd's Oilettes, posted in 1904 in Braintree, Essex. Artistic cards had sales everywhere.

end of the market amongst the self-styled artistic photographic studios. On the back of their cards, they printed little advertisements for themselves, which were often so fancy and decorative that they are more attractive than the rather boring studio photograph on the front. A&G Taylor, who had studios in Sunderland and South Shields, so they really were hot shots, announced on their cards that they were 'artists in Platinotype, Bromide and Carbon'. Sounds terribly impressive, but what was Platinotype? Don't tell me. I'd rather it remained a mystery. They also claimed to be 'The largest photographers in the World', but then lots of firms claimed that.

Tuck, with their Oilettes, commissioned a well-known Victorian artist called S.T. Dadd to do drawings for a series called Football Incidents, such as 'A Close Shave', and also an Oxford v. Cambridge game. His status as a proper artist is recognised by the fact that Tuck gives him a credit on the card, 'after the black and white drawing by S.T. Dadd', which was unusual.

Other firms did similar series, illustrating other incidents, such as 'Well Saved', showing a goalie punching out the ball. In that 'Well Saved' card, the crossbar looks a bit improvised, so it must have been at that stage between tapes and proper fixed crossbars.

FOOTBALL INCIDENTS.
CHARGED THROUGH (Association).
After the black & white drawing by S. T. DADD.

one that a player is about to catch. Could it be prophetic – an image of Thierry Henry 101 years before he handled the ball against Ireland?

Postcard artists who only did postcards naturally did not achieve the eminence or acclaim of real artists, producing real paintings in the conventional sense, but some postcard artists did achieve a certain fame in their own field, such as Alphonse Mucha, Raphael Kirchner and Louis Wain. Their postcards were highly valued and people collected them to put in postcard albums or on their mantelpieces, rather than post them through the post, and they are greatly prized today. Mucha, for example, was a noted graphic artist and one of the pioneers of the art nouveau movement.

Alas, the better postcard artists used their talents on more obviously artistic topics than football, preferring to do landscapes, views, gardens and fashions, or they did decorative and highly stylised graphic work for hotels, holiday resorts and railway companies. Football, by its nature, did not

by the National Football Museum). It is from the cover of one of the best ever football books, *Association Football and the Men Who Made It* by Alfred Gibson and William Pickford, published in four volumes in 1903. A set of these books has pride of place on my football bookcase and this simple image, which is on the spines as well as the covers of all four volumes, follows me across the room, watching me.

Over the decades, some quite well-known real artists, from Picasso to L.S. Lowry, have painted football scenes, but as paintings, not postcards, though often they have later appeared as postcards. Several watercolour artists have also done paintings of football scenes, trying to capture the atmosphere. Cecil Beaton, the photographer and designer, did an interesting oil painting in 1955 showing a goalie making a save.

Henri Rousseau did a painting in 1908 called *Les Joueurs de Football (The Football Players)* but it looks a bit surreal and the ball a funny shape, the

A 1930s poster by J. Petts of a goalie. Both this and the above book cover were later turned into postcards by the National Football Museum.

ART, FASHION, POLITICS 161

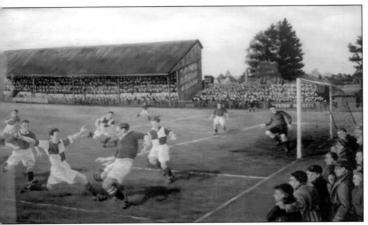

Paintings as postcards.

Above left: Watercolour by E. Prater, 1913. Left: Oil by William H. Pearce of a Man Utd–Bristol Rovers game, 1953.

Above right: Homemade artwork, but professionally printed, of two church or college teams, 1908.

lend itself much to artistic interpretation. Football fans wanted to see their teams and heroes in real photos, not arty-farty oily things.

I must admit that when I am looking through dealers' boxes of football postcards, or football cigarette cards, I tend to avoid the caricatures or the drawings, unless they are very old, in which case age makes them appear more interesting. The artwork on the football postcards of the 1920s and 1930s was cheap and derivative, most of it influenced or copied from football cartoons in the national newspapers.

The result of this is that you don't find in football postcards the various artistic styles and fashions, such as the arrival of art nouveau, that you can trace with other sorts of postcards. You see the changes in football playing – in the teams, the stars, the strips – but not in the style or artwork in which they are represented.

Now and again people did try to produce their own personalised version of an artistic football card, without much success. I have a card, professionally printed, for it has 'POSTCARD' on the back and stick your halfpenny stamp here, but the picture itself looks as if some amateur or perhaps a student has done it. It portrays a match between Sinjuns – presumably short for St John's – and St Mark's and is dated on the back 1908. It is about a real game that finished 4–2. It's amusing, but puzzling.

OGDEN'S CIGARETTES.

W. BEATS.

OGDEN'S CIGARETTES.

J. LEWIS.

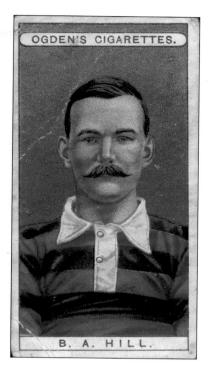

OGDEN'S CIGARETTES.

B. A. HILL.

OGDEN'S CIGARETTES.

T. BADDELEY.

OGDEN'S CIGARETTES.

NEW BROMPTON.

How to get ahead in football: get a 'tache. Some fine examples from Ogden's Famous Footballers cigarette cards, 1908. Beats played for Wolves, Lewis for Brighton, Hill for Blackheath and Baddeley was a Wolves goalie. The New Brompton player is not named as the series he came from was called Famous Club Colours.

K. WILLINGHAM, Huddersfield Town.   TOPICAL TIMES

E. CATLIN, Sheffield Wednesday.   TOPICAL TIMES

Topical Times cards, 1930s. Big format, horrible colours, but great middle partings.
Willingham's hobbies were golf and billiards.

Were they two church teams? Or theological colleges battling it out? What did the birds in the trees mean and the devil-like figures?

Fashions amongst footballers, as opposed to fashions in artwork and graphics, are clearly reflected in cards of all sorts over the last 120 years. Strips and shin guards we have done, but facial hair, its rise and fall, is an area well worth some really detailed study, perhaps a PhD at the Leeds Metropolitan University.

As I have a moustache, and have done for about 30 years or so, I am always interested in historical moustaches – who wore them and what were the main styles. Young footballers, even in the days when they did not have much money, liked to see themselves as fashionable men around town, wearing the latest caps, spats, shoes. Their hairstyles reflected what was in fashion at the time for men of their age.

Ogden's produced a set of Famous Footballers in 1908 in which the definition of fame, in order to get into the set, almost seems to have been a spiffing moustache. There really were some splendid examples, but the more I look at them, I become suspicious that there were in fact only two moustaches – one turned up slightly twirled at the ends, using Vaseline or similar, and the other a bit droopy. A lot of them look pretty false, as if on the day of the photo shoot that was all they had in the studio box, so all the players had to take a turn at wearing one of them.

In the 1920s and '30s, many men wore a middle parting, but footballers' middle partings seem to have been more extreme, more dramatic than the ordinary man in the street's, especially when, as in the *Topical Times* cards, they appear to be touched up and colour tinted to make them more glamorous. Wouldn't happen today, would it?

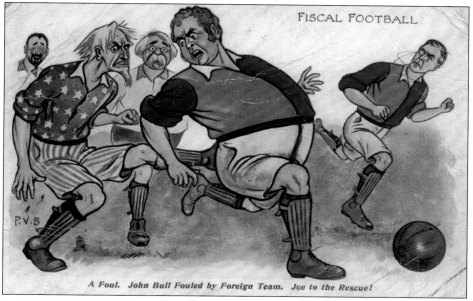

Political cards. Above: John Bull is being kicked by Uncle Sam and other foreign baddies, 1906. Joe Chamberlain, running on the right, has a monocle, if you look carefully. Below: Joe is in goal, saving us from foreign goods.

"OUR GOALIE HAS NEVER BEEN THE SAME SINCE HE WAS AN AIR RAID WARDEN. EVERYTIME HE SEES ANYTHING COMING HE DUCKS."

Political and topical references: Above, 1940s, when air–raid wardens were in the news and below, Tom Browne's take on, er, tariff reform, free trade, politics possibly?

A. THROW IN.

Lib—Lab get stuck in, 1890s.

Political football cards combine clever artwork, the ability to catch a likeness, an understanding of current political dramas and a working knowledge of football – which probably explains why as a subgenre it is not exactly a crowded field.

Leaflets and posters have traditionally been the mass means for politicians to get across political messages, and political cartoons in the newspapers have been the weapons used to mock and cut them down to size. There's not much that postcards can add politically that can't be done better elsewhere.

However, there have been occasions when postcards have been used to get across a political message or at least comment on a political topic of the day. In 1906 – judging by the postmarks – Tuck produced a series of cards called Fiscal Football. The story in the news was a protectionist campaign run by Joe Chamberlain, the government's Colonial Secretary, against foreign imports, to give our colonies more security. So foreigners were seen as a menace, trying to crash in, using dirty tricks, the sort of behaviour that could easily be transferred to the football field, with a bit of licence.

I find it hard to believe that everyone, even at the time, got all the political jokes and references. One card shows John Bull being fouled by a foreign team, so that is pretty straightforward. Joe Chamberlain is the one with the monocle, while the nasty foreign attackers include Uncle Sam, the one in the shirt with stars on. I think. Not sure who the other figures are, but they must have represented real characters of the day.

The artist's initials are given as PVB. He was Percy Venners Bradshaw (1877–1967), a well-respected and long-established artist who worked a lot for Tuck and most of the main magazines. He was also a teacher and had founded the Press Art School.

The postcards, judging by the postmarks on the back, were published in 1906 – which was the year poor old Joe Chamberlain suffered a stroke. He remained an invalid till his death in 1914.

A rival company, Tamesis, produced a card with a similar theme at about the same time, in which Joe is in goal – you have to look hard to see his monocle. He is wearing a Union Jack strip, while the Yankees and other baddies are trying to kick foreign foods into his goal.

An even earlier political card using a football theme came out in the 1890s, which makes it one of the earliest football-related political cards. I'm not quite clear about the message, but I'm sure it was awfully clever. A ball marked ILP – for Independent Labour Party? – is being headed towards goal, while another ball is marked Liberal–Labour. In the background you can see the Houses of Parliament, while the crossbar is marked Boro, as in Middlesbrough.

The First World War produced a few cards with football and politics mixed – one showing the *entente cordiale* with Britain and France kicking a ball that is meant to be the Kaiser. In the Second World War, the best I can find is a goalmouth scene with the goalie missing the ball. The caption explains that the goalie had been an air-raid warden. 'Every time he sees anything coming, he ducks.' Well, it was topical.

Tom Browne, the well-known postcard artist, uses the football phrase 'a throw-in' as a caption for a scene of some yokels throwing someone in uniform into the water. It was presumably making some clever comment on a political story of the day. Tariff reform? Protectionism? Free trade? Agricultural subsidies? Land reform? Dunno. I am only a simple football fan . . .

It all comes out in the wash: Spurs' laundress hangs out the team's kit, 1935.

Chapter Fourteen

Der Höhepunkt.

Prachtige omhaal.

FOOTBALL ABROAD

Football got exported very early on, which I suppose is not too unexpected when you realise it was a period when Britain was exporting almost everything – factories, industrialisation, railways, clothes, goods, services, engineers, civil servants, workers and pastimes. And with almost all of them, pretty damn soon those foreigners were making or doing them or playing them much better than we were.

Our economic and industrial dominance led to our culture, not just our goods, being exported and accepted abroad, but all the same, the speed with which certain aspects of our national life got immediately adopted in foreign fields is still very surprising – especially football. It was as if for several centuries they had been sitting waiting over there for us to invent the rules, create the terminology, think up the strips, mark out the pitch, then whoosh, the moment they heard what we had done, they were off, on the park, up the field, scoring spectacular goals. Even before we had properly got ourselves organised, before obvious things like leagues and professionalism

had started, while we were still mucking around with the rules, our football had spread like swine flu around Europe.

Football arrived in Denmark, Holland and France in the 1870s – before we had got round to shin guards, whistles, goal nets, two handed throw-ins and penalty kicks. In fact there are reports of football being played as early as 1860 in Lausanne in Switzerland. In 1863 in Paris, France, a newspaper reported people playing footer in the Bois de Boulogne.

Arguments about which was the first club in Europe still go on, because some of the early ones do not exist any more and the very early ones were also cricket clubs, so do they count? Their members played a bit of knockabout football in the winter months, before eventually football became their main game.

France's oldest football club is generally agreed to be Le Havre, formed in 1872, but originally the club was for athletics and rugby, with the association game taking over later. In Denmark, their oldest football club was founded in 1876 –

Brits took footer round the world. In 1908 the crew of the SS *Sidra* played a game against another ship and when they reached New York produced a postcard naming the whole squad.

Европейская война. АНГЛІЙСКАЯ ДѢЙСТВУЮЩАЯ АРМІЯ. Военная футбольная команда.

Репродукція воспрещена

изд. фот. "Идеалъ" Невскій 112.

An English touring team in Russia, circa 1920s. AFA possibly stands for Army Football Association. Great postcard, but who were they and where?

Copenhagen Boldklub, now merged into FC Copenhagen.

There were two basic sources for the foundation of almost all the early European and also South American clubs – and both came from the UK. First of all there were the upper classes, officers and gentlemen who found themselves in some far-flung colony or outpost and naturally wanted to continue life as they knew it, regardless of the local conditions, culture or climate. Hence they began sports clubs, playing either cricket or football. At the same time, ordinary British workers, building factories or railways abroad, or British soldiers and sailors fetched up on some foreign soil, would start kick arounds and create their own teams.

The Le Havre club was formed by visiting British sailors. In Switzerland, the game was imported by British boys at finishing schools, who went on to help found Swiss footer clubs with English-sounding names, such as Grasshoppers of Zurich and Old Boys of Basel. In Italy, local British residents began the Genoa Cricket and

Football Club in 1892, and in Milan in 1898 the Milan Cricket and Football Club was formed, later called AC Milan. Note that the spelling is not Milano, as in Italian, but always Milan, which is the English version. In Spain, some British workers began a club in Bilbao in 1893, while in Scandinavia the first football games were played by Scottish shipyard workers.

Sometimes foreign teams also based their strips on British teams. Juventus of Italy today play in black and white because when they were setting up, Notts County gave them a set of their strips.

In most of these European countries, they had established their own FA by the 1890s – Denmark was 1889, Switzerland was 1895, Belgium 1896 – and had started their own league system around the same time.

South America followed almost as quickly, its earliest clubs dating back to the 1890s. British railway workers in Uruguay formed their own sports club in 1891, while the first local team of Uruguayans was started at Montevideo University by an expat English professor. Brazil

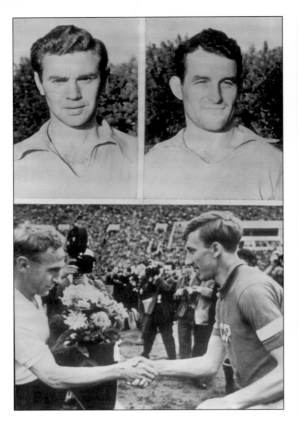

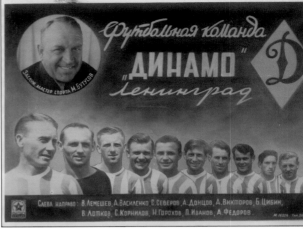

The Russians always issued lots of cards of their top teams, like Dynamo Leningrad (above right, 1930s) and Moscow Dynamo.

Above: Two Russian stars and below Billy Wright, 1958 England captain, shakes hands with the Russian captain.

Below right: Yashin in cap, famous Russian goalie, 1957.

first tasted football when the Royal Navy visited, and probably a few other delights too.

As in Europe, many South American clubs still sport English-sounding bits to their club names – Old Boys, Racing Club, Juniors, Corinthians. Such old-fashioned names reek of the influence of the public school amateurs who began our FA. These were the sorts of chaps who were very quickly off touring abroad. Once they heard about all these footer clubs being set up by expats

in exotic places, they packed their togs and set sail, to play exhibition games, spread the word, enjoy a nice long cruise in hot weather and a bit of a jolly for a month or two. Being amateurs, they did not need to hurry back.

Corinthians, the famous amateur club, played 23 games in South America in 1897, while Queen's Park of Glasgow toured Scandinavia in 1904. Southampton, in 1904, were the first professional club to tour in South America.

One of my favourite postcards shows a football team in 1908 from the ship's crew of a liner called SS *Sidra*. They are in full football gear, taken somewhere on land rather than on board. Each person in the photo has been carefully numbered and their name, rank, and position on the field written carefully in very neat handwriting on the

back. Two are described as 'supporters present at Teneriffe match', which suggests they had played a game there, and that was perhaps where the photo was taken. The card itself was posted in Brooklyn, New York, on 13 December 1908, and sent to a Mrs Miles in Gateshead, County Durham. I love the idea of them cruising round the Canaries, then over to the USA, playing a football game in whichever port they docked.

The team consisted of stewards, cooks, bosun, engineers and other crew members. The referee is named as Captain Hood – numbered 9 in the photograph, who is wearing a jaunty, rather American-looking hat – and it says he was from SS *Gretavarde*, which I assume was a rival ship, possibly the one they had just played against.

I also have a card showing an English team in Russia, having played against some Russian team. I am waiting for some good Russian speaker to translate it for me, but I am guessing it was an English team, as the goalie is wearing a jumper that says AFA – for Army Football Association or Amateur Football Association?

Early postcards of what are now famous European professional clubs, the sort who regularly give our lads a thumping, are hard to find, or else collectors in Europe hold on to them. Whatever the reason, I have rarely seen them at British fairs or auctions. I think, though, that football postcards, like football programmes, were never as popular or as common in Europe in the early decades as they were in Britain.

Most of my famous European clubs are Russian for some reason – and most of them show Moscow Dynamo or perhaps Leningrad Dynamo. This is partly because during the Communist era, the Soviet government was keen on postcards, leaflets and posters as a means of propaganda, so they were produced cheaply in large numbers. A club like Moscow Dynamo was world famous and reflected well on the Soviet Union. They issued countless sets, some showing Dynamo or the national team in action or coming out before a game. They also feature Russian stars, such as Yashin, or English stars, such as Billy Wright in 1958 about to lead England against the Ruskies.

German teams.

Above: Augsburg–Ingolstadt, 1917.

Below: An unnamed team, circa 1900s, strike a pose. Was the player on the ground the captain trying to look cool or was he just knackered?

Moscow Dynamo was the first foreign club I was ever consciously aware of. I remember the excitement when they came to Britain for a short tour in 1945 to cheer us all up after a long war. They seemed so exotic, so unusual, so foreign. That's how I recall it anyway – cutting out their photographs from the newspapers and sticking them in homemade albums with homemade paste

alongside my favourite Scottish players. We were living in Dumfries at the time. No wonder they seemed exotic.

They played football in an unusually disciplined, well-drilled way and attracted massive crowds wherever they played. There were 90,000 at Ibrox to watch them play Rangers and draw 2–2. Against Chelsea (score 3–3) there were 85,000 at Stamford Bridge. They beat Arsenal 4–3 before a crowd of 54,000 at, wait for it, White Hart Lane. Yes, this is a trick question I often use to catch out Gooners. The match couldn't be played at Highbury because the ground had been taken over for war and military reasons, so Spurs kindly let them borrow their ground.

While I don't have any pre-war cards of the famous Spanish, French, German or Italian Big Teams, I do have lashings of their Great Unknowns. For the same thing that happened in Britain happened in Europe, almost from the beginning of organised football. Once a season, a team would have its photograph taken and cards made to be sent to friends and relations.

As in Britain, they usually lined up in three rows – forwards, midfielders, defenders – but, ah ha, for some reason, they preferred a slightly different order. Instead of 5-3-3, which they should have used, dear me, if they were properly copying their brothers in Britain, they arranged themselves as 3-3-5. For example, you often see the goalie sitting in the middle of the front, not in the back row, with, I assume, the full backs beside him. The five at the back are presumably the forwards.

As in Britain, there were always teams trying to be fancy dans, arranging themselves in an unusual line – with some players lolling on the

French and Belgian teams.

Above: 1909, no name, but groovy shirts and socks.

Middle: Nice bikes and berets, but no sign of the onions.

Below: Theux, 1905. Founded in 1901, still playing in Belgium.

ground at the front, attempting to look cool, despite some of the fans trying hard at the back to get into the shot.

Quite a few of the German teams seemed fond of standing in the goalmouth, while a very young German team in 1910, F.M. ATV – assuming that was their name – are looking extremely neat and organised in 3-5-3 formation, with their goalie in the middle at the front with two players leaning against him.

Almost all my old French sporting clubs are unknown, I think, even the one with the bikes against the wall. Sporting Club de Theux, seen in a 1905 postcard, are still a well-known club in Belgium.

I don't have many European football stadiums, except for Barcelona. I am told that European football fans are mad keen on postcards of stadiums, so perhaps they rarely reach these shores.

Outside Europe, I have come across lots of postcards of teams from India, the Middle East and elsewhere, though some might in fact be British military teams, stationed abroad. The exact location and country is not always clear, but I pop them in the India or Africa files if the background strikes me as vaguely tropical. On one South African card, someone has written on it 'Bloemfontein', which is useful.

I have two black teams – one not named, but it has a white man sitting in the middle who could be military, so probably some sort of army team. The other is dated on the front 'February, 1946, Takoradi, Gold Coast, S. Africa'. The names of all twenty-two players in the sepia photo are recorded on the back – indicating there were two

Brits abroad.

Above and middle: The same club, possibly a wartime army team, as they look so thin. A dog makes the picture in one, an Indian–looking boy the other.

Below: Definitely Bloemfontein, South Africa, 1918.

Gold Coast, South Africa, 1946. Two black teams, possibly military, who have just played a game: black shirts against yellow shirts.

different teams, as opposed to one large squad. One team was called All Blacks – who played in all black – while the other team, named as 5 WA Field Ambulance, played in yellow shirts and shorts. If you look carefully, you can see the two different types of strips. The game ended 2–2. You don't often get notes on the back so informative.

Once again, as in Britain, comic cards quickly followed the mass passion for football. When it comes to illustrated cards, there is a definite European style. The artwork on the whole is better and in the comic cards they don't seem as influenced by newspaper cartoons and caricatures as the artists in Britain. They are more stylised, more like book illustrations.

But they fall into the same rough types as in Britain. The very early artistic cards showing football scenes are Oilettes, or sometimes colour-washed or tinted. You also get football scenes being used for advertising purposes, promoting things like chocolates.

Now and again there are some interesting wartime references. One very early Belgian card shows some soldiers playing football on a beach watched by some nurses. It might have been some sort of charity card – in the sense of proceeds going to charity – as on the back it says, 'Asilis Des Soldats Invalides Belges'.

A much more modern card, also from Belgium, shows two captains about to kick off, hiding their guns behind their back. The message is pretty clear – Make Football, Not War.

One of the most artistic foreign cards I have I bought in 1989 at an exhibition of Latin American art at the South Bank Centre. It shows a three-dimensional football team from Brazil, made in clay and then painted. I wish I had the original.

I recently read a feature on the current Brazilian team – now doing brilliantly once again. But when Dunga originally took over as manager, the team did badly and he was very unpopular. In 2008, the front page of Brazil's *O*

Prachtige omhaal.

Der Höhepunkt.

Les petits désagrément du foot-ball

Artwork abroad. As in the UK, there were painted scenes and loads of cartoons.

Above right: Dutch, circa 1890s.

Above left: Also Dutch.

Middle right: In French but posted in Germany, 1917.

Middle left: Looks Dutch.

Below: A French card posted to Chelsea, London, 1909.

FOOTBALL

Globo sport section had a mock obituary of the team, complete with a large black crucifix. The headline over the team photo went as follows:

> Brazilian football, winner of Five World Cups, communicates the death of Dunga's national team in Belgium, China. The Seventh-Day Mass will take place on Friday, 8 o'clock, in Shanghai Stadium. Please, do not send flowers.

Never seen it as a postcard, alas, but it proves that In Memoriam jokes are still alive in foreign football.

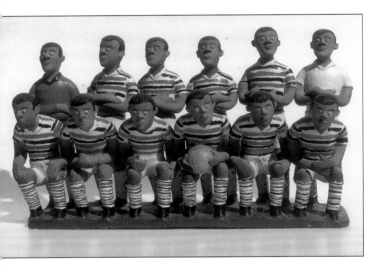

Above: Make football, not war, this Belgian card, circa 1950s, seems to be saying.

Below: Clay figures of a Brazilian team, 1970. Published by South Bank Centre, 1989.

Chapter Fifteen

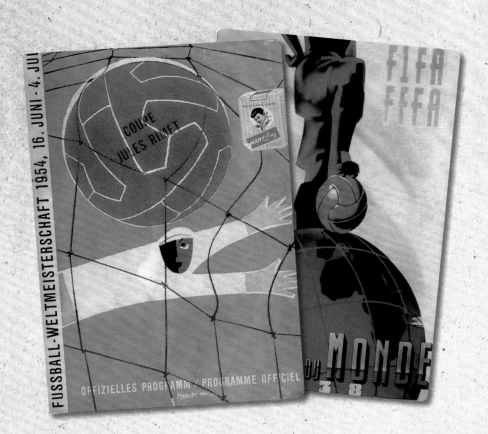

WORLD CUP

FIFA, the world governing body of football, was created in 1904 by seven of the leading European countries where football had first flourished – France, Belgium, Denmark, Holland, Spain, Sweden and Switzerland. Spot the odd ones out. Yup, the FAs of England, Scotland, Wales and Ireland said up your bum, we are not joining, it's our game, we began it, you can have your own organisation, see if we care.

From the early years, there was talk of a World Football event in which countries from all over the globe would take part, but there were always arguments or complications caused by the refuseniks such as England.

However, football was first played as an official sport at the Olympics from 1908. England won the gold medal in that first year and also in 1912. I don't actually recognise any of the England players in that 1912 postcard, but they were England amateurs, who of course could still show the amateur world how to play. On their shirts they don't have a lion, or three, but the Union Jack, as England was representing Great Britain.

In 1928, the Olympics were held in Holland and I have a postcard before the final showing the two captains, of Uruguay and Argentina – and also, more interestingly, the referee and linesmen for the final. Just look at those outfits. Natty or what? I assume the three officials were in different gear because they came from three different countries and were sporting whatever it was that smart or top refs wore in those countries at that time. I wonder if there is someone who collects referees on postcards? Bound to be.

Football at the Olympics has not always had an easy passage. In 1932 it was dropped after a row over expenses from the South American teams, and then in the 1936 Olympics, held in Germany, there was trouble over certain teams who said they had been forced to give the Nazi salute.

Uruguay won the Olympic gold for football in 1924 and 1928, and it was partly due to the euphoria of this, and the fact that in 1930 the country was celebrating a centenary of its independence, that in 1930 they offered to

England's team, winner of the football gold medal at the 1912 Olympics, held in Sweden. Note the Union Jack – they were representing the UK.

Natty refs line up before the final of the 1928 Olympics, held in Holland.

57   DE AANVOERDERS, SCHEIDSRECHTER EN GRENSRECHTERS URUGUAY—ARGENTINIÉ

hold the first World Cup – and pay the expenses of those who took part. Only four European countries took up the offer – France, Belgium, Yugoslavia and Romania.

The king of Romania picked his country's team and managed to get them all off work so they could go. The four European teams travelled on the same boat, which took two weeks, keeping fit on the decks. Jules Rimet, the French lawyer who was president of Fifa, was also on board, carrying the World Cup itself in his luggage.

In all, thirteen countries took part, including the USA. There were mutterings that the US team included some professionals from Scotland. Wouldn't have done them much good today. They did get to the semis but were beaten by Argentina, who met Uruguay in the final.

Before the game, they argued about which ball would be used. A compromise was reached whereby the Argentinian ball was used in the first half – by which time they were ahead 2–1 – and the Uruguayan ball was used in the second half. Uruguay went on to win 4–2, which proves something or other.

Those two match balls from that very first World Cup of 1930 have now been united at England's National Football Museum (which was at Preston but is opening again soon in Manchester). The museum had had the Argentine ball for some years, but only recently received the Uruguay ball on a long-term loan from a private collector. Footer fans can now ogle both balls together. I have done so, and can report that the balls are indeed slightly different, with the panels in different shapes. One ball looks a bit bigger and is missing the lace and one is slightly more orangey than the other, but I have now forgotten which one it is.

World Cup posters, cards and images have usually been of a higher quality than normal football artwork.

Left: 1954 World Cup, Switzerland.

Right: 1938 World Cup, France.

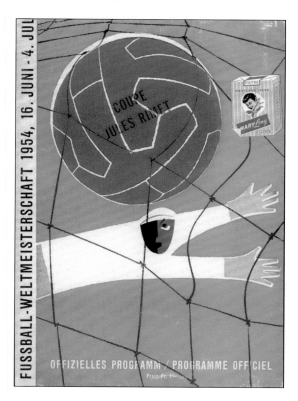

The next World Cup was held in 1934 in Italy, establishing the principle that the World Cup finals should alternate between South America and Europe, which continued till 2002, when Japan and South Korea were hosts. In 2010, South Africa became the first African nation to host it.

Meanwhile, back to the early World Cup years. Our FA was forever faffing around, changing its mind, agreeing to join FIFA in 1924, then leaving again in 1928. At its 1928 meeting, one FA member, Charles Sutcliffe, was dead against the whole notion of FIFA.

Above left: 1942 South America championship.

Above right: 1934 World Cup, Italy.

Below left: Argentina, 1978.

'FIFA does not appeal to me,' he said. 'An organisation where such football associations as Uruguay and Paraguay, Brazil and Egypt, Bohemia and Pan Russia are co-equal with England, Scotland, Wales and Ireland seems to me to be a case of magnifying the midgets ...'

England finally agreed to join FIFA after the Second World War, in 1946, in time for the 1950 World Cup in Brazil, where they were humiliated by the USA, 1–0 in the first round. The USA was a country not supposed to know anything about soccer. That was a shock, but we have had several since.

One very good thing about World Cups has been the artwork. On the whole, the official posters, postcards and logos produced by each host country have been excellent, commissioning some of the best graphic designers and artists of the day, especially for the World Cups of 1930 and 1934, plus 1938 (held in France), 1950 (Brazil) and 1958 (Sweden). Most of the original posters also later appeared as postcards. But there

Above: Discreet Royal Mail postcard for 2002 World Cup in Korea and Japan – the first World Cup finals not held in either Europe or South America.

Below: one of a set of postcards for the 1958 World Cup, Sweden.

UDDEVALLA

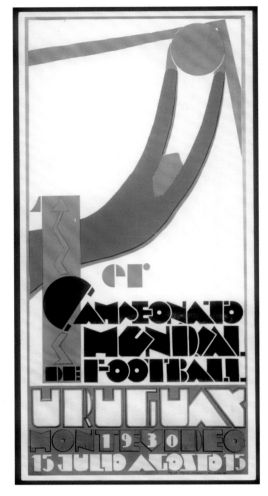

Above: Proof that Scotland used to be a regular World Cup finalist: Mexico, 1986, as lovingly remembered by the St Vincent Philatelic Services.

Left: Postcard commemorating the 1930 World Cup, Uruguay.

were special sets of postcards issued at the time as well, as in Sweden in 1958.

England's use of World Cup Willie as our mascot when the World Cup was held here in 1966 was possibly not our finest artistic hour, though the lads did good on the pitch. For the 2002 World Cup, our Royal Mail played safe with a very discreet World Cup postcard.

For recent World Cups, there has been a flood of postcards produced all round the world by different post offices, even by countries who never took part, their own post offices deciding to cash in by issuing their own World Cup postcards and stamps.

For the Mexico World Cup of 1986 – won by Maradona and Argentina, who beat Germany 3–2 in the final – there was a flood of postcards throughout the world – which was fortunate for Scotland. Their presence at the 1986 Mexico finals – their fourth successive World Cup appearance in the finals – has been immortalised on a postcard produced by the Philatelic Services of St Vincent in the West Indies. A shame Scotland got knocked out in the first round, winning only one point. There could well be some followers of the Tartan Army still stranded out there in St Vincent, clutching their postcard, too embarrassed to come home.

Chapter Sixteen

MODERN HEROES

Who would have ever expected horny-handed, poorly educated, scarcely cultured working-class blokes who kicked a ball around for a living to be knighted? Certainly not those well-bred, amateur, pukka public school types who first played our football and then ran it for so many decades. All it took was a hundred years. Quick, really.

Stanley Matthews, in 1965, was the first professional player to be honoured. All the heroes before him, all household names in their times, who burst nets and burst records, must have been sitting up there thinking, where did we go wrong, why didn't we get a gong, or even a decent wage? On second thoughts, once they had perused the Stanley stats, they would surely have agreed that his knighthood was well deserved. There were wizards of the wing before him, and a few afterwards, who hugged the touchline, confused the lumps with his fiendish body swerve, did mazy dribbles, but we won't see his particular like again. Hugging the wing and mazy dribbling is now a hanging offence with modern coaches

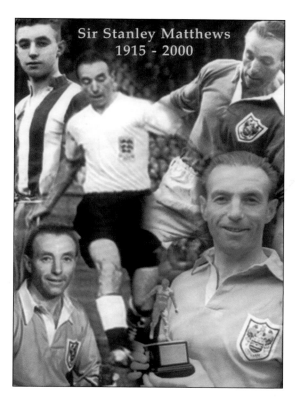

Sir Stanley Matthews
1915 - 2000

Five footballing knights on a limited—edition card by Football Postcards Collecting Club, 1995: Stanley Matthews, knighted 1965; Alf Ramsey, 1967; Matt Busby, 1968; Walter Winterbottom, 1978; and Bobby Charlton, 1994.

– you have to tuck in, get back, cover, fill the hole, help your full back if he goes forward, do what you are told and belt up.

Matthews also set records for standards of behaviour on the pitch, an example to all, known and revered around the world, the very symbol of what English fair-play football was all about – supposedly. In a professional career lasting 34 years, he never got booked. In 1956, he was voted the first ever European Footballer of the Year. His knighthood came when he was still playing, going out on the park, doing his stuff. Again, it is hard to imagine such a thing happening in the future.

Matthews played at a time when there was a maximum wage – £8 a week when he began, slowly rising to £20 a week in 1958. When the maximum was abolished in 1961, it was too late

for him really, as his peak was over, and anyway it was another 30 years before players' wages began their spectacular rise. For almost all his playing life, he was never above £20 a week – but being a star, a household name, he did make himself another £20 or so a week by letting the Co-op use his name.

He died in 2000 – but postcards featuring him still come out when people are honouring the greats and the very goods of the past.

Stanley Matthews was not technically football's first knight, for several football officials had received honours before him – Sir Charles Clegg of the FA in 1927, Sir Frederick Wall in 1930 and Sir Stanley Rous in 1949. Rous had been a very modest player, but achieved fame as an outstanding referee before becoming secretary of the FA and president of FIFA.

Once a real, professional player like Matthews had got knighted, other players followed, though either long after they had retired – like Sir Bobby Charlton in 1994 – or after they had become better known as successful managers, such as Sir Alf Ramsey in 1967, England's World Cup-winning manager, and Sir Matt Busby in 1968, manager of Manchester United, the first English club to win the European Cup, in 1968 (but not the first British club, as Celtic won it in 1967). Sir Walter Winterbottom also got knighted. He had played for Man United and Chelsea, but achieved more fame when in 1946 he became England's first ever manager – before that, a committee had been responsible for the team.

All these five football knights, honoured in a limited-edition card produced by the Football Postcard Collectors Club, were at their heights, as players or managers or administrators, in the period between the 1950s and the 1970s – yet this was the beginning of one of the worst ever eras in English football.

It's hard to believe it now, but there was a period not long ago when English football appeared washed-up, knackered, not much good you know, its days numbered.

Immediately post-war, it had all seemed so rosy, with massive crowds flocking back, having been deprived of all league games during the war, desperate for entertainment and distractions and excitement. Just before the war, in 1939, English league football had been attracting 28 million a season. In 1946–47, attendance shot up to 35 million. In 1948–49, it reached 41,271,424 – a record that still stands to this day.

Then it was a slow, worrying downhill slope. By 1956, it had dropped back to 33 million. In 1964, it was 27 million. Despite the World Cup win, it continued to fall during the '70s. Then came the lowest point of all when in 1985–86 it dropped to 16,488,000. That was well under half what it had been before the Second World War. So what had gone wrong?

The post-war euphoria had exaggerated the state of football, making it appear healthier than it was. In the '40s and '50s, there was virtually no TV and people did not have cars or take foreign holidays. There were few rival attractions and distractions or competition for our leisure time. Then in the 1970s came the scourge of football hooliganism, which drove many supporters and their families away. In crowd shots of those years, you hardly see any women, perhaps fewer than there had been in the 1920s.

The standard of our football appeared to decline, other countries were winning all the pots and plaudits, our expectations got lower, people had become less interested. Football had fallen out of favour and flavour. Learned committees were set up to look into the state of football.

In 1984, after 112 years, the annual Scotland–England games were abandoned, events that had captivated both nations, along with the other so-called Home Internationals. I don't think my heart has ever beaten as loudly as it used to do when I was little boy listening on the radio to Scotland play England.

The act of going to a game had become pretty horrible. You stood on nasty, open, windswept terraces or crouched in rickety Victorian grandstands, with rubbish food and smelly open lavatories. Some desperate and pathetic measures were tried to brighten up English football, such as plastic pitches, but were soon dropped.

The single most important event that helped modernise football, to bring it back to life and into our national culture once again, was the Hillsborough Disaster of 1989, when 96 people were killed and 150 seriously injured during the Cup semi-final in Sheffield between Liverpool and Nottingham Forest.

The resultant Taylor Inquiry recommended all-seater stadiums, which many administrators and fans were sceptical about, but with government help and backing, it was eventually done. Almost all our leadings grounds were rebuilt or modernised to become all-seater.

By 1992, crowds had returned to the 20 million mark. Today they average about 30 million. It's unlikely they will be as high again as 1949, when almost everyone at a football match watched while standing. Architecturally speaking, the

WITH THE COMPLIMENTS OF Ty·Phoo LTD., BIRMINGHAM 5
TEA

TOTTENHAM HOTSPUR F.C.

Back row, L to R: Baker, Norman, Brown, Blanchflower, Henry, Mackay
Front row, L to R: Jones, White, Smith, Greaves, Dyson

Spurs, League One winners 1960–01, just the team, not hordes of the squad,
sitting beautifully, arms folded, legs apart – a full–colour goodie from Typhoo Tea.

theory they work on is that only one person can sit where previously two could stand.

Old Trafford, Britain's biggest club stadium, is now enormous and holds 76,000, and so is the Emirates, with its 60,000 capacity in a fabulous new arena. At one time, many so-called lesser clubs, like Blackburn, Bolton or Sheffield Wednesday, also regularly had gates of 60,000 to 70,000 – almost all of them standing. While total league gates have dropped, the income generated by the Premiership is about 100 times what the First Division produced pre-Second World War.

The second big reason for the success of English football has been the advent of satellite TV, particularly Sky TV, and the huge amount of money it has poured into football, particularly since it bought the rights to the newly created Premier League in 1992. Much criticised, much regretted at the time, but it is now obvious that the billions they have poured into football – using it as their main marketing and sales strategy – has shaped the nature of and helped create the success of the game we see today, making the English Premiership the most watched league around the world. So Sky tells us all the time, so it must be true.

Today's stars have made a quantum leap, not just by becoming millionaires, which even journeymen players in the Premiership now become, but by turning into celebrities, icons, envied and adored, accepted by all classes, invited everywhere, to the best parties, the best houses, from Downing Street to stately homes, asked for their wisdom, their input, their presence or at least their name.

Images of today's golden boys are everywhere, in advertisements, commercials, magazines and on all sorts of cards – but postcards, of the sort we

Two recent England stars, each on a National Portrait Gallery card. Left: David Beckham, photo by Lorenzo Agius, 1998. Right: Bobby Charlton, oil by Peter Edwards, 1991.

have always known and loved, bought to post to each other, are not as numerous as they once were and are usually produced directly or indirectly or in co-operation with commercial sponsors. The days of normal postcard manufacturers being able to run off a few hundred thousand copies of a series called Famous Footballers or Famous Clubs, as they used to do pre-war, have gone. They have to pay, to get permission from the Premier League, from Man United or wherever, all of which can be costly.

That yummy-looking photograph of a young David Beckham taken by Lorenzo Agius in 1998 was issued by the National Portrait Gallery – and sold to support the National Portrait Gallery, so a very worthy, rather than a commercial, cause. As was the fine oil painting of Bobby Charlton, painted in 1991 by Peter Edwards, which the gallery owns. The fact that it was the National

Portrait Gallery that issued these two cards – and did them beautifully, he added quickly, bijou works of art – is an interesting sign of the times, proof that modern footballers are part of both high and low culture, their portraits hanging in such a distinguished place.

I have another nice card of a modern-day icon, Eric Cantona, that has an art-gallery connection. I picked it up for free, as it was advertising a touring exhibition in Tullie House, Carlisle.

The FA itself regularly issues lots of individual postcards of the England players and officials. I was given a whole set when I went to visit someone at the FA in 2006. This was when Steve McClaren was manager, remember him, ably assisted by Terry Venables. On the backs of the cards are listed the FA's partners. People they sleep with? Folks who help to pick the team? Nope.

Terry Venables
Assistant Coach

ENGLAND

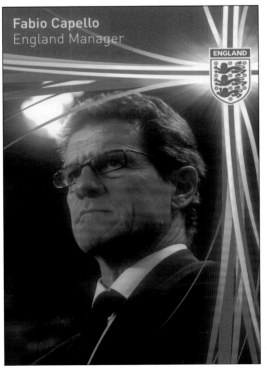

Fabio Capello
England Manager

ENGLAND

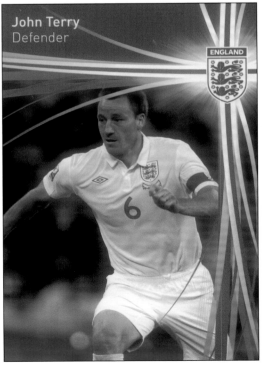

John Terry
Defender

ENGLAND

Steven Gerrard
Midfielder

ENGLAND

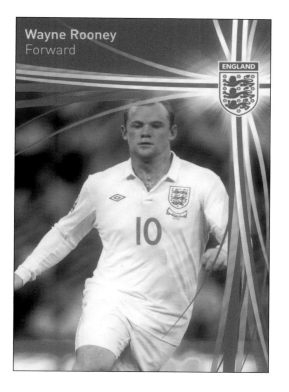

Wayne Rooney
Forward

ENGLAND

Frank Lampard
Midfielder

ENGLAND

David Beckham
Midfielder

ENGLAND

Brazil, 1958 World Cup winners, not all looking directly at the camera.
Pelé is third left in the front row.

Spurs 1951 League One champs, all direct. Alf Ramsey, left in back row.

ENGLAND FOOTBALL TEAM 1981
Back Row, left to right: Trevor Francis, Viv Anderson, Phil Neal, Trevor Brooking, Peter Withe, Russell Osman.
Middle Row, left to right: Bryan Robson, Paul Mariner, Peter Shilton, Phil Thompson, Ray Clemence, Glenn Hoddle, Peter Barnes.
Front Row, left to right: Ray Wilkins, Mick Mills, Tony Woodcock, Kevin Keegan, Terry McDermott, Kenny Sansom.
Photograph: BOB THOMAS © Football Association

The squads start growing: England lads, all 19 of them, in 1981.

All it means is that they are big firms who have given them money. Their names and logos are all there on each card – Nationwide, McDonald's, Umbro, Carlsberg, Pepsi. We postcard collectors are naturally very grateful for their input.

But all praise to the FA, who recently kindly sent me a set of our 2010 World Cup heroes. They don't charge a penny for their cards, seeing it as a service to football. All you have to do is write off to them, tell them how much you love all the England players and you could be lucky.

When it comes to team shots, you really need large-format postcards these days as the squads have grown so huge. After the Second World War, in the '50s and '60s, official team photos looked much as they ever did, with the first team in two or three rows, arms folded, the cup or ball in front. That magnificent 1958 Brazil team that won the World Cup, beating Sweden 5–2 in the final, with the young Pelé, Garrincha, Vavá and Didi, managed to get their arms folded in the back row but were less organised in the front row, all of them on their haunches, with Pelé looking down, not at the camera.

The Spurs team that won the double in 1961 were a bit more formal and have a bench for the front row to sit on. All eleven of them did what they were told, got their arms folded the correct way and each one smiled for the camera.

From the '80s onwards, team shots tended to include the whole squad, as in the England group of 1981, which featured 19 players. By 2006, with Sven in charge, the official England squad had expanded to 24 players. In Europe, the same sort of thing was happening. The Barcelona squad of 1989 shows 31 – but that included coaches and staff and possibly a few people who had wandered in from the crowd.

And growing and growing: Barcelona (above) in 1989 managed 31 for their team shot, while England (below) in 2006 had grown to 23 – plus Sven.

A more beautiful game

Katie Chapman, Midfielder.

now go play | TheFA.com/women

England women stars, now supported by the FA. Katie Chapman, tough–tackling Arsenal midfielder, moved to Chicago Red Stars in 2010.

The large squads reflect the numbers of players, usually 23, that can now be named for the big events, such as World Cups and European Championships, and also show that in ordinary league games, the squads are now about the size of small armies.

Up to the '70s, a club programme would name the 11 players only, numbered 1 to 11 in the middle of the programme, surrounded by adverts, with a blank left for the twelfth man 'to be announced'. Only one sub was allowed, whose name you could fill in on the day. In the '80s, the numbers went up to fourteen, as two subs were now allowed. (Not thirteen – that is eleven and two subs – as many clubs don't have a number thirteen because that is considered unlucky.)

By the 1990s, squads had grown to about 20 and the team names had moved from the middle to the back page of the match programme. Today they practically need a separate supplement as the squad numbers can go from one to fifty. I have the programme for last week's Arsenal home game and their list of players goes up to 54, Sanchez Watt. Nicklas Bendtner, who was usually getting a more regular first-team outing, was number fifty-two. It must take a computer to keep track of all the shirts and kit.

At present, three subs are allowed to come on, but you can name seven as subs waiting on the bench. That is one reason for the increased size of the squad and the bench. The management

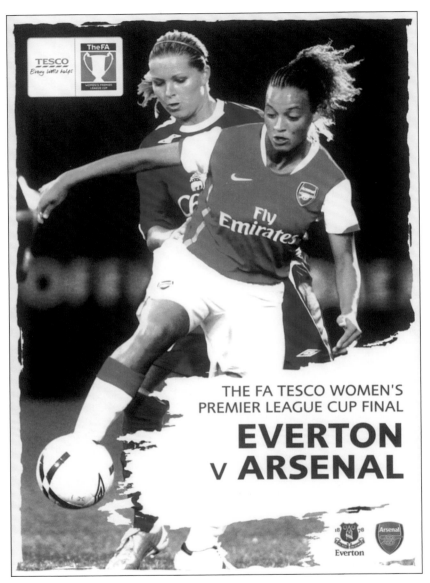

Women's Cup finals attract around 30,000 spectators. In 2010, Everton beat Arsenal 3–2 in the final.

and coaching squad has also grown enormous so benches are now about five tiers deep and look like the gallery at the National Theatre.

Our heroes today now include heroines, for women's football, having suffered the ignominy of being banned by the FA in 1922, is now a world force, more popular than it has ever been.

The Women's FA was formed in 1969 and in 1971 it was officially recognised by the FA. In 1993, the FA itself took over responsibility from the Women's FA, which is still the case. The FA looks after the teaching and coaching, and over 16,000 women have now taken FA coaching qualifications. Around the country there are 52 Centres of Excellence for women. The FA reckons there are now 260,000 women regularly playing some sort of football in England and 1.1 million girls aged eight to sixteen.

The growth abroad has been even more remarkable, especially in the USA, Germany, Norway, France and China. The Women's World Cup was held in the USA in 1999 and 90,000 turned up to watch the final. The American players became household names and their star player was said to be getting $100,000 a year. The problem in England has been getting sponsorship and decent TV exposure, though Cup finals have attracted audiences of around 30,000. Still not as high as Dick Kerr Ladies in 1920.

In England, there is a Premier League for women, plus two lower leagues, North and South, and also a Cup. Only a handful so far have ever made much money out of the game in England. The best they have usually been able to hope for is a coaching job at somewhere like Arsenal, allowing them at least to train full-time.

The first women's international in the UK was between England and Scotland, who else, in 1972 – the England women won 3–2. England has made it to two World Cup finals, in 1995 and 2007, but they didn't progress far. Their best success so far came in 2009, when they reached the final of the European Nations Cup.

Ten years or so previously, when I watched the occasional women's game on TV, I could see they

Katie Chapman
Midfielder

ENGLAND

Katie Chapman – official FA card.

were enjoying playing, but thought it would never catch on as a spectator sport. It was too slow, clumsy, amateurish. Today, the improvements have been remarkable, partly because of all the FA coaching courses and also the stars polishing their skills and power in the USA. Quite a few of the England stars now play full-time professional football in the USA.

Watching the 2009 women's final, I found it skilful, exciting, technical, fast, furious and physical, for the women have now learned to do crunching tackles and shirt pulling, just as the men have always done. They can strike a dead ball, deliver solid headers. A shame England got beaten in the final by a really excellent German team, but they received great praise and attention and the FA then decided to put 17 of the top women on proper contracts, thus enabling them to give up their day jobs and concentrate on football full-time.

What is really surprising is that figure of over a million girls now playing football – and it has taken off amongst all classes and from a very young age. A neighbour of mine, a top barrister, is thrilled that his eight-year-old daughter Bells now trains with Arsenal's under-nine girls, even though it means a huge trek each week to their training ground in the wilds of Hertfordshire.

One of my relations, a girl aged ten, plays for Yeovil Ladies Under-12s. I had been hoping for a photo of Lily in the team, expecting any day to receive a postcard. Eventually it came – by email. Better than nothing. She looks so proud, sitting in the team shot, in three rows, as nature ordained.

Football teams of all sorts and levels still do have their photo taken each season in the traditional way, but ordinary teams up and down the country no longer seem to troop into studios or get a professional to print proper postcards. They all have instant digital cameras and immediately send the images off round family and friends on the Internet. How will posterity have permanent records or families have proper images to treasure?

I fear these modern times could spell the end of postcards of Unknown Teams, the sort that were produced at one time in millions. People are now using the Internet, not the post, for so much of their communication. Letters have all but disappeared. Pity the poor biographers in years to come with no handwritten material to draw upon.

Thank goodness for famous teams and famous players. If anything, their images are even more popular and valued than ever before, by all sorts of people, for all sorts of reasons.

Chapter Seventeen

MODERN TRADING

My ten-year-old granddaughter Ruby has just come into my room and painstakingly explained to me, as if I was a total idiot, about the 2010 World Cup Match Attax cards. 'You what?' I said. 'Never heard of them.'

'Oh Humpa,' she said, which is my nickname, a combination of Hunter and Grandpa, 'let me explain.

'You buy a packet in a newsagent's for 50p, which has six different football cards in it. If you are lucky,' she said, 'you find a silver one, which is really precious, then you swap any doubles with your friends and get the ones you haven't got . . .'

'You mean trade cards,' I said. 'I collected them as a lad, only we didn't call them Match Attax, now what were they called, let me think. They have been going for at least 120 years . . .'

'You are not that old, are you Humpa?'

Each generation of boys and girls thinks stickers and trading cards are a brand-new and exciting format, which they become obsessed by for a year or so, perhaps just a season, or even a few weeks, even half a day. Excitements do come thick and fast these days and rarely last. About the only element that appears to be new is that you can track down cards you haven't got on the Net. Mr Baines never thought of that one.

Trade or trading football cards – which you buy in packets and then trade your doubles – does, as we know, go back as far as Baines, but perhaps they existed even earlier, in some form or other.

Sometimes they are called stickers, because you stick them in a specially prepared album, and such cards are usually flimsier cards with nothing printed on the back. Otherwise they are known as trading cards, which are heavier and thicker and more like playing cards and postcards. You just collect them, trying to get a set, then do whatever you do with trading cards – leave them around to get lost is usually the answer.

Stickers are a much better concept with more commercial possibilities, as you do end up with a proper artefact, a solid-looking album, which usually has loads of relevant information on every page, surrounding the stickers you have just

Some modern stickers by Match Attax, 2008 – keeping up the tradition of collecting packets of them begun by Mr Baines in 1890.

stuck in. It means, of course, you have to buy the album, not just the stickers, again something Mr Baines does not appear to have thought of.

I have two completed albums of Panini stickers from 1981 and 1982, which I bought a year ago at a car boot, just because there was so much in them: seventy-two large-format pages crammed with mug shots of every player in both the English and Scottish First Divisions, plus team photos and club crests, and also details on each club in the lower leagues. There must be almost eight hundred stickers in each one – a bargain at ten pounds each, when you think of the money that must have been spent and the hours of labour, I mean fun, putting it all together.

The man I bought them from, who had collected them himself as a boy, back in the 1980s, said that really he should be charging me fifty pounds each, but he was hard up. I didn't quite believe him. I mean Panini stickers are really trivial, flimsy, juvenile, childish things, aren't they? Not proper, historic, solid things like, well, postcards.

The Panini brothers grew up in Modena in Italy. In 1943, they were running a news-stand in the town when they decided to branch out and sell

little packets of football stickers. In just a couple of decades, they were turning over billions of lira. In 1988, they sold out to the Maxwell Group. A decade later, they were bought by an Italian conglomerate. Today they still operate as Panini and their factory and world HQ are still based in Modena. They have been in the UK since 1978 and today their UK office is in Tunbridge Wells. When I rang them there to ask some questions, they couldn't tell me very much, referring me to Modena, who referred me to their website. According to that, they have 700 employees in 100 countries and are the biggest producers of stickers and trading cards in the world – covering pop and film subjects as well as football.

There are of course many rival firms doing similar sorts of things, such as Match Attax, which is part of something called INtoys, based in Liverpool, and also Topps, Merlin and Ava – though some of those names may be part of the same group. They all seem very reluctant to talk about themselves, perhaps worried about rivals knowing their plans and methods.

What is clear is that the sticker and trading-card business is now enormous. The simple act of kids buying a little packet of football stickers for a

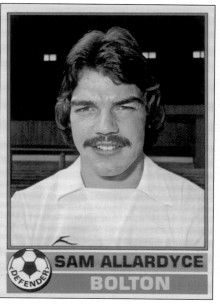

SAM ALLARDYCE
BOLTON
DEFENDER

JACK CHARLTON
LEEDS UNITED
CENTRE HALF

More stickers. Above, left to right: Post—war version, Billy Liddell, 1940s and '50s star of Liverpool and Scotland, produced by Chix Bubblegum; Sam Allardyce, 1970s, from Topps Chewing Gum; Jack Charlton, 1960s, from ABC.

Right: Cristiano Ronaldo, 2006, from Magix Box Inc.

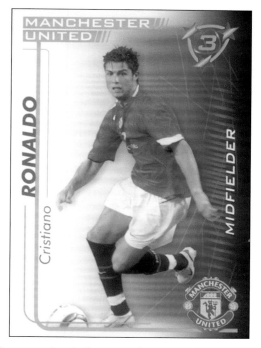

few pennies has developed into a global industry generating millions and employing thousands of people.

Trading old, second-hand stickers and albums has also become a business, but I suppose I should not be surprised by that. I contacted Andy Firr in Wallasey, who runs Classic Football Stickers, which has been going for 30 years. He said that the most expensive old sticker album is the Panini one for the 1970 Mexico World Cup, which can go for £1,000, complete. Even an empty one can be worth £500. A series of FKS stickers called the Wonderful World of Soccer Stars from 1967 is also very desirable. Panini albums from the 1980s, that is before the Premier League, are now going up in price, and certain years can fetch £200. So the man I bought mine from was not lying. Yes, Mr Baines would be quite amazed if he came back now.

Post-war football postcards, meanwhile, don't command the prices of some post-war football stickers, nor have they morphed into a massive global industry. Ordinary postcard manufacturers find it very hard to compete in the football market,

Modern trade cards, given away by Adidas.

Above: Mick McCarthy, Ireland manager, 2006, before the World Cup.

Below: David Beckham commemorating, hmm, an England free kick in the last minute of a World Cup final. I wish.

unless they have some sort of tie-up with the top clubs or the leagues or are printing on behalf of some commercial organisation.

But trade cards – meaning cards produced to promote in some way some sort of trade or product or commercial enterprise – are a thriving business. Most of the big football clubs have their own postcards, showing their latest squad every season, which are sold in the club shops, but usually the sponsor's name is very prominent, giving away the trade connection.

Postcards of individual players usually also carry a sponsor's name, discreet or otherwise – as do postcards of managers. Alex Ferguson can be seen in a Man United shirt on which Vodafone is writ large – which, of course, is not there any more, as sponsors move on even if some managers don't. Manager Mick McCarthy's face might not quite be as recognisable on an Adidas card, nor is the quote 'Reputations? Bring 'em on' quite as clear as it was in 2006, when little Ireland were going to the World Cup finals.

The big advantage of all these football postcards connected in some way with a sponsor or some commercial outfit like Sky TV is that you can usually get them for free, either when they are given away at sponsored events or by simply writing to your fave player or manager, asking for his photo, and the chances are he – or at least his agent's office – will send you back a lovely glossy postcard of him looking really smooth and handsome. A high-class photographer will have been used and the card produced by his current sponsor, which, of course, sees it as part of their marketing and promotion. You couldn't do that in 1900 or 1930, as of course players were not tied to brands or sponsors. You had to rely on the comics for your free cards. There are some advantages to this modern world.

The disadvantage in this rise in importance and power of the sponsors is to the media rather than the ordinary humble fans collecting postcards of their heroes. Football hacks and reporters now find it almost impossible to gain easy access to our star players. In the old days you could hang around the car park and get ten minutes with any or all of them, without an agent or manager or lawyer in sight, or ring them up at home. Today everything is totally controlled. In every TV post-match interview you can see all the sponsors and names of the partners lined up on the walls and screens behind.

For a proper interview, or even just a few minutes, the press has usually got to rely on

SKY SPORTS
Live Barclays Premier League

THE **HEROES** SEASON

MANCHESTER UNITED

vodafone

ALEX FERGUSON

More modern trade cards. Above: Cesc Fàbregas of Arsenal – thank you, Sky Sports.

Left: Alex Ferguson of Man Utd – and Vodafone, a big hug.

events or press conferences organised by the player's sponsor, when, say, a new boot is being launched, or when an exercise video is coming out with which they are connected. Selected journalists are then allowed into the player's presence – on the condition that the product is properly plugged and they don't ask too many personal questions, such as why the player was seen falling out of a club or why they hate the manager and do they still want a transfer?

Now and again players and clubs also do things for charity, so in this case a worthwhile cause is being plugged. Restrictions still apply. But it is true that most Premiership players do spend some time each week in hospitals or doing some sort of charity work. Well done them.

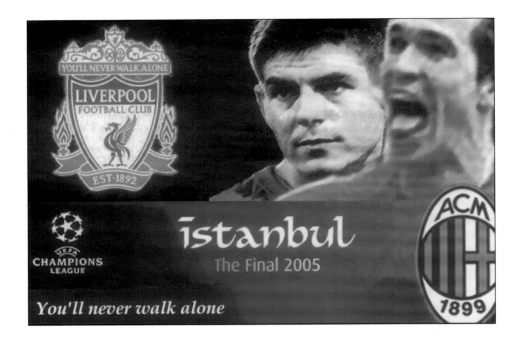

Some modern events on postcards.

Above: Liverpool's Euro Champions League win in 2005.

Below: Euro Nations 1996, held in England.

As well as players and managers, big events are still commemorated on postcards, such as Liverpool's famous victory in the European Champions League final in Istanbul in 2005, when they came back from the dead to beat AC Milan. England hosting the Euros in 1996 produced quite a few postcards.

Stadium cards still appear, though not as many as before the Second World War. In some ways they are more impressive and revealing than in the past, thanks to wide-angle lenses. They are usually sold by the club shops and can range from the big new architectural wonders like Arsenal's Emirates to Brunton Park, home of the famous Carlisle United – well, famous in my house – or little old Chesterfield FC. They did a card in 2009 to mourn the end of the Recreation Ground, Saltergate, which had been their home since 1871 – making it the world's oldest football ground occupied by the same tenants. At the start of the 2010–11 season they moved to a brand-new ground with a really brand-new awful-sounding modern name – b2net. Bolton Wanderers also did a commemorative card when they left their old home, Burnden Park, in 1997.

You might expect *The Sun* and the other tabloids to be producing lots of giveaway football cards as promotional tools, just as popular newspapers did before the war, but the best set in recent years was issued in 2009 from *The Guardian*. They came with serrated edges, which slightly spoils the look of them, but the photographs are all excellent, showing famous football scenes and events of recent years. Many of the photographs, such as Brazil celebrating beating Scotland in 1982, were taken by the newspaper's own photographer, in this case Eamonn McCabe.

The interesting thing about *The Guardian* using football cards as a promotional tool is that it is a sign of the increasing participation of the professional classes in football, something that hardly existed or was not very apparent before the war. It can be argued that you have to be fairly well-off to afford to go to football games these days, as a season ticket for most Premiership clubs will cost you around £1,000, so many of the working classes can't afford

Euro '96: a rather artistic card produced by MasterCard, one of the official sponsors.

it, but it is also because following football has cut across all classes and ages.

I often go to Arsenal with a friend of mine who is a judge, someone I have known for 40 years. When he was younger, I don't remember him ever talking about football or going to games. It was through his children that he became interested. When they grew up and left home he kept on his season ticket, as he found he loved it so much. All politicians now boast that they follow football – and with most of them it is probably true.

Football does now link ages and classes and races together in a way it never did before. In most social and intellectual circles, if you start a conversation on football, you'll find people joining in, giving their wisdom. In pubs, it has always provided conversation – though today it is not always possible because of the noise of the giant telly or rows of giant tellies blaring out the live match.

Modern stadiums — well, nearly.
Above: Arsenal's Highbury, which closed in May 2006.
Below: Saltergate, home of Chesterfield till 2009.

SALTERGATE - The Home of Chesterfield FC

Free postcards given away by *The Guardian* in 2009, showing famous World Cup scenes of recent years. Above: Becks gets sent off in France, 1998, Popperfoto. Below: Brazil celebrating beating Scotland, Spain 1982, photo by Eamonn McCabe.

More *Guardian* cards. Above: Kevin Keegan misses a header, Spain, 1982, photo by Eamonn McCabe. Below: Chris Waddle misses a penalty, Italy, 1990, photo by Mike King.

Chapter Eighteen

MODERN GREETINGS

Greetings cards using a football theme are still with us, especially for birthdays and Christmas. All my family for years have given me a birthday card with a footer element somewhere, which does save them having to think of what to get for me. Some are a bit naff and yucky, particularly for some reason the ones produced abroad, as in France. I suppose we are too cynical and self-aware and rude to go in for the sort of sentimental slushy ones that the Victorians loved.

Lots of greetings cards reuse old football photographs, such as the two pre-war players standing in the snow looking at the ball before kick-off, which is a nice festive motif and something you don't see any longer now that our pitches have under-soil heat and other tricks to keep them mud- and snow-free. This particular Christmas is a charity card, produced by Card Aid.

A lot of them, as in the past, are meant to be funny, but of course these days using computer technology. I have a clever one with my name on a

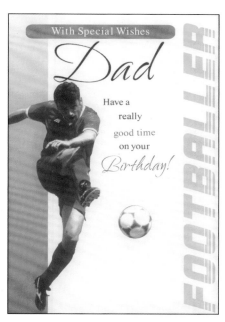

Really corny birthday card with footer image, not much different really from those done 100 years ago, from my dear daughter Flora when I was, oh . . . only last year.

Modern footer cards have the benefit of being able to use old images.
Above: 1930s snow scene, produced for Card Aid.
Below: Computer enhancement managed to get me into the England dressing-room.

Right: 3D image of Martin Chivers, Spurs and England, produced by *The Sun*, 1970s. One of a set of fifty.

Below: Already a collector's item – the National Football Museum is now moving to Manchester. The old ball is the Uruguyan one used in 1930 World Cup final.

shirt hanging up in the England dressing-room, along with Gerrard, Owen and so on.

Gimmicky cards are not seen as often as they were before the Second World War – when cards often had pop-up and pop-out bits, or separate inserts. Back in the 1970s, the *Sun* newspaper did a series of 50 3D cards – so not greetings cards, as such. They were pretty good and they did seem three-dimensional, even without wearing any special sort of spectacles.

There are lots of little companies and bodies who do produce their own football cards from time to time, promoting their own little brand or humble events or just to say hello, present themselves, greet the world.

Books and films and exhibitions that have a football-related element often produce a one-off postcard with a football image in order to promote themselves. The National Football Museum greets visitors with its own postcards, of itself, which are for sale. The one giving its address in Preston is already an historic card – as the main museum is now being moved to Manchester.

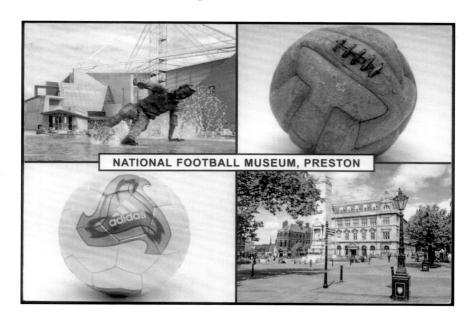

NATIONAL FOOTBALL MUSEUM, PRESTON

A POMONA BOOK

kicked into touch
(plus extra-time)
FRED EYRE

Manchester City, Lincoln City, Huddersfield Town, Crewe Alexandra, Buxton, New Brighton, Quarry Town, Bradford P.A. Chorley, St Helens Town, Southport, Wigan Athletic, Bury, Stalybridge Celtic, Northern Nomads, Radcliffe Borough, Cheadle Town, Ellesmere Port, Chadderton, Rossendale United, Sheffield United, Stockport County, etc. etc.

Left: The story of an ex–Man City apprentice, published by Pomona Books, 2005.

Below: Clever title. A Sheffield United fan's story, from Juma, 2001.

Charity cards still exist, or cards pushing causes as opposed to commercial concerns, such as the Sue Ryder Care or action groups who are running a campaign trying to get their message across. In 1991, an action group calling themselves TISA – Tottenham Independent Supporters' Association – issued postcards showing Gazza and Gary Lineker, whom they didn't want transferred. Some messages, once the event has passed or the cause has been forgotten, are now quite hard to follow – or perhaps they were just statements, in the air, not tied to an event.

The postcard of the new Wembley being built as glimpsed from a train station was produced in 2004. I bought it at a postcard fair, thinking it was an offbeat way to feature a new architectural wonder and cultural icon – but now I turn it over, I see it was privately produced by a couple called Roger and Adrienne Lee. I rang Roger up, to check it was OK to use it, and of course it was fine. He turned out to be a Methodist minister

who was retiring from Wembley to Bicester, so he was using the card to announce their new address to friends and colleagues – hence the Bicester signpost. 'It was the day they were putting up the arch, so I just caught it. The station with the Bicester sign has now been rebuilt – so you couldn't take that photograph today. I got 200 cards printed to send to friends, hoping it would catch their imagination.' So it is a greetings card, to greet their friends. Clever, huh? And also a limited edition. Well done, Rev. Roger.

There is a card produced by a firm called Boomerang Media of Aldershot which has the slogan 'Football Dementia' and shows the inside of a brain obsessed by football, morning, noon

FEVER HITCH

ADRIAN BELL

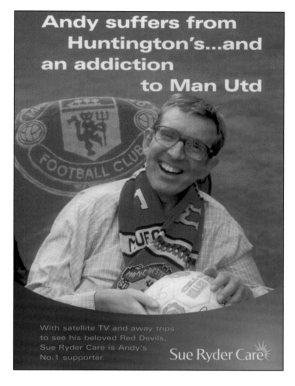

Andy suffers from Huntington's...and an addiction to Man Utd

With satellite TV and away trips to see his beloved Red Devils, Sue Ryder Care is Andy's No.1 supporter.

Sue Ryder Care

Left: Charity card from Sue Ryder Care.

Below: Not so charitable, in that the card was issued by Spurs Independent Supporters in 1991 to protest at the club's AGM about possible sale of Gary Lineker and Gazza.

and night. It's a giveaway card by a media firm who produce those free cards you see in cinemas, schools and universities these days to promote a film or service or whatever. In this case, they were just doing a bit of artwork to promote themselves, not any business or trade. The message on it is almost identical to one produced exactly 100 years earlier, in 1910, which also illustrates 'Football on the Brain' – only this time a cloth-capped fan is shouting 'Goal!', with a footballer perched on the top of his head.

I have also, boast boast, received club Christmas cards from well-known players and also from managers and officials at various clubs. Most football clubs, like most big organisations, have their own Christmas cards these days. In some cases, if you join their junior supporters

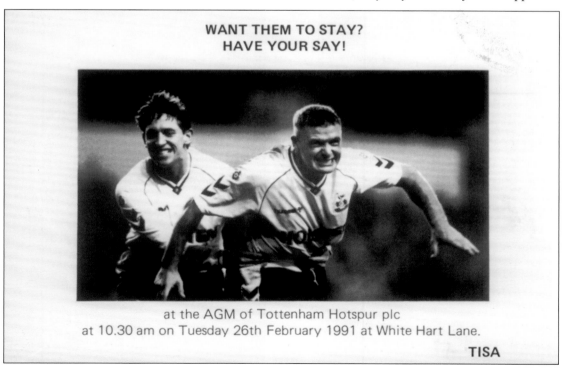

**WANT THEM TO STAY?
HAVE YOUR SAY!**

at the AGM of Tottenham Hotspur plc at 10.30 am on Tuesday 26th February 1991 at White Hart Lane.

TISA

Above: The new Wembley arch going up in 2004, taken by Rev. Roger Lee as a change–of–address card.

Below: A hundred years apart, the same message
– football on the brain – 1908 and 2008.

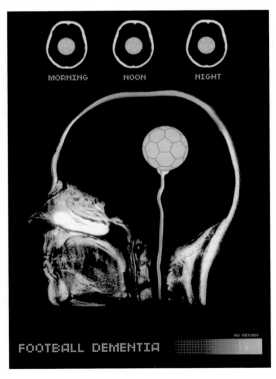

club you will receive a club greetings card on your birthday or at Christmas. Exciting, huh?

I have quite a collection of these club Christmas cards and other people must now be doing the same, for you often see them in local auctions. Some are pretty boring, as they just use the usual festive scene on the front and could be from anyone, with a message from the directors inside, but many are specially done individual cards related to their club, which might have their squad photo on the front, such as with Everton or Arsenal. Some put their minds to it, hire a photographer, fancy clothes, create a scene and produce unique and funny personal cards. I have had several from Spurs over the years, who always do excellent Christmas cards. The England team have also done good ones that appear to show just the usual squad line-up, till you realise they have

Club Christmas cards. Right: Spurs 2007 Christmas card, using 1963 scene of snow being cleared off the pitch by a fan before a Cup game. Below: Spot the Santa: England team under Graham Taylor, 1992.

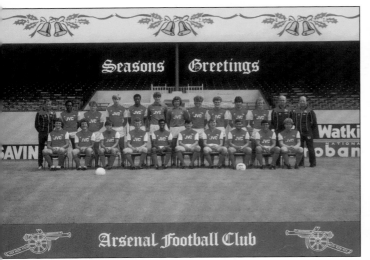

incorporated a Father Christmas figure, usually one of the players dressed up. You have to guess which one it was. In the old days, it was often Gazza. Shows they are human.

When Joe Kinnear was manager at Wimbledon, he sent me a Christmas card showing caricatures of himself, Sam Hamman, the owner, Vinnie Jones and other players. Inside it sent best wishes from the Crazy Gang at Selhurst Park Stadium.

That too is now an historic card as of course that Wimbledon Football Club, as we knew it, no longer exists.

Top left: Boring, straight-faced Christmas card from Arsenal, 1983, unlike Spurs (top right), with Santa in the dressing-room.

Above: Period piece from Wimbledon FC — 1990s Christmas card with manager Joe Kinnear, right, chairman Sam Hamman, plus stars. Now the club is no more.

Chapter Nineteen

FOOTBALL POSTCARDS TODAY

The days of postcards as the main means of mass communication have gone. People communicate, wherever they are in the world, by computers and email, by mobile phones, by tweeting or texting or Blackberrying, or whatever is the latest fad, rather than by sending a postcard. Stuck in a foreign part, buying a stamp is hard enough, as is finding a post office or post box, but then there is the worry of when it will get there, if ever.

Yet a hundred years ago, postcards were as popular as emails and mobile phones, and with deliveries several times a day in urban areas, you could communicate quickly and safely with your friends or loved ones.

Best of all, you had something to show at the end, something which was special, personal and unique, not like a boring old text message. People appreciated and valued their postcards, retaining and treasuring them, rather than immediately deleting them from their machine, from their minds, from their life. Old postcards are now collectors' items, for millions of them never faded away, got lost or destroyed or forgotten.

It is estimated that one third of the population is a collector, which means about twenty million people in the UK. The success of such programmes as the *Antiques Roadshow*, the rise of eBay, the huge increase in car boots and collectors' fairs, shows the popularity of collecting generally.

Postcard collecting is only one part of it. And inside that part, collecting topographical cards – usually starting with cards of your immediate area – is the most popular single form of postcard collecting. After that, transport, social history and sports probably rank next – with football making up one of the elements of the sports section.

And yet in football-postcards collecting, we do have our own society, oh yes, the Football Postcards Collectors Club, with its own journal. Along with suffragette postcards, which happen to be one of my other interests, football-postcard prices have shot up hugely in the last ten years. At one time I could buy a pre-war postcard of Spurs or Man United for £8. Now it is at least £40, often nearer £80.

The world's most expensive footer card sold at auction: £1,057 paid in 2009 for this 1920 card, the earliest known image of Dixie Dean – middle front row – in football kit.

One of the highest known prices for a football card so far is £1,000 – which was paid recently on eBay for a 1910 postcard of the Old Trafford stadium, the first year that Manchester United played there.

Part of the reason for the increase in prices is, of course, the rise of postcard collecting generally. There are now so many of us around – and so many places and ways to buy cards. We are spoiled for choice and variety and places and people from whom to purchase.

The UK's best-known and biggest postcard fair is the monthly Bloomsbury Collector's Fair, which takes place in London on the fourth Sunday of the month at the Royal National Hotel in Bedford Way, Bloomsbury. It was set up in 1977 by Clive and John Smith and is now run by Phil Smith and his brother Dave, who also produce the annual *Picture Postcard Values* catalogue, which lists 6,000 different cards from around the world.

I was overwhelmed when I first started going about twenty years ago by the sheer size and scale, with postcard dealers as far as the eye could see – and beyond, for in those days it took over two large function rooms. In all there used to be 200 tables and 100 different dealers. Today, there are normally around 100 tables and 50 different dealers, but even so, I always wonder where to begin and worry that I'll never get round them all. Each month, around 1,000 collectors turn up, hoping to find treasures.

'We are still the biggest postcard fair by far,' says Phil Smith, 'but the reason we are not as big as we once were is because there are now so many of them. When my dad, Clive, began, we were about the only monthly fair in the whole country, so we got dealers coming from all over. Now, instead of one dedicated postcard fair a month there are about thirty – some big and some fairly small, but they are in all parts of the country. Dealers and collectors don't have to travel so far these days.'

Brian Lund, based in Nottingham, is the editor and publisher of *Picture Postcard Monthly*, which has 10,000 readers every month. He also publishes books about postcards and runs regular postcard fairs in Nottingham. He reckons there are around 500 postcard dealers in the UK – though not all of them do it full-time.

Earliest known image of Dixie Dean — second row, sixth from right — in an Everton shirt, 1924. Sold by Graham Budd/Sotheby's for £705 in 2009.

Professional postcard dealers, doing nothing else, probably don't number more than 20.

'I did think when eBay arrived, and then the recession, that postcard fairs and dealers would have a hard time, but I am surprised by how well everyone is doing. There seem to be more postcard dealers and collectors coming into the hobby all the time,' he says.

There are also more and more auction houses that hold specialist postcard auctions, though most of them these days are in the provinces, such as Warwick & Warwick in Warwick and Trevor Vennett-Smith in Nottingham. At one time, the big London auction houses like Christie's did do specialist postcard sales, but they have ceased. However postcards do still appear at auctions at both Christie's and Sotheby's.

Graham Budd, who runs sporting memorabilia auctions in association with Sotheby's, says the market for football postcards has always been good. 'The most desired are cards from the Golden Age, by which I mean pre-1920s – and it's the famous British teams and portraits that make most money.'

In October 2009, he broke the auction-house record (as opposed to an eBay sale) for a football postcard with one showing Dixie Dean, which went under the hammer for £900 – or £1,057 after the auction house's 17 per cent was added on. It shows Dixie Dean, aged 13 or 14, in a boys' team and is the sort of football team card I have dozens of, showing fresh-faced young lads lined up in the usual pose – five at the front, three in the middle (though one is not quite in line) and three at the back, with the goalie in the middle. These are the ones I look and think, hmm, I wonder if any became professional footballers, or millionaires, or murderers.

It was very clever of someone to work out that one of them is Dixie Dean, for all that the caption underneath the team says is 'W.J. McCulloch, 561 New Chester Road, Rock Ferry'. It was in fact Birkenhead Boys Club during the 1920–21 season. The attraction of the card is that it is the earliest known image of Dixie Dean in football kit. He sits in the middle of the front row, ball at his feet, and was presumably the captain. Even in this rather faded group shot, you can see that he did have black curly hair and a darkish complexion – which later led to his nickname. When he first

Postcard by Stuart Clarke, the leading producer of proper football cards today.
Rangers fan in a Gazza mask at Hampden Park, 1996.

turned out for Tranmere, the crowd called him Dixie, a convoluted reference to the Southern states of the USA, from whence he did not come, but the topic was currently in the news.

At the same sale, another of Dixie Dean in a different group photo, a few years later, in 1924–25, when he had just recently joined Everton, also fetched a lot of money – £705, including commission. The point here was that it is the earliest known shot of him in an Everton shirt. I suppose if you are a diehard collector of Everton memorabilia with enough money – and the most fanatical fans tend to spend most on their favourite club – then when an unusual and possibly unique postcard of one of your heroes comes up, you feel you have to have it. Which I quite understand. Collectors collect.

Modern football postcards are still being manufactured, although not as many as before, and the market is splintered between scores of different companies, groups and organisations, producing football cards for their own reasons, usually connected with advertising something or other.

Up until the Second World War, there were still dozens of postcard artists, designers and photographers who did nothing else except produce football postcards, but as a profession or a craft, they have all but disappeared.

However, there is one modern-day photographer, Stuart Clarke, who does specialise in football postcards, and who happens to be an artist in his own right. He has revolutionised the art of football postcards, producing, so I believe, some of the best football postcards ever, taking them to new heights with the quality and imagination and technique of his work.

Stuart Clarke was born in Hertfordshire in 1961. He went to a public school, Berkhamsted School, which Graham Greene once attended, then to the Central London Polytechnic to study art and photography. Afterwards, he wandered around the globe for a bit, trying to decide what sort of photographer he wanted to be, before getting work with the magazine *Time Out*. In 1989, they sent him one wet weekend on a job to Glasgow and it was there a thought and a phrase struck him that transformed his life.

'I could see how much football mattered to the people of Glasgow and it struck me that this was one of the Homes of Football. I began to think of all the other Homes of Football, all over the country. The Hillsborough Disaster had not long happened, so perhaps this was in my mind as well. I decided there and then that this was what I was going to specialise in from now on – photographing the Homes of Football.'

From the beginning, he didn't go for the obvious football shots – the star players and the goalmouth action. He concentrated on the stadiums, the fans inside and outside the ground and, most of all, the atmosphere.

He held little exhibitions of his photographs in various places over the country, before realising it would be better to have his own permanent gallery.

'I looked at various places, such as Wigan. The council was trying to encourage artists and little businesses to set up in Wigan Pier, but there were so many problems and not enough help. I decided I would have to go it alone, not rely on others.'

He was already living in the Lake District, having first hitch-hiked there in 1985 and never left, and decided to look locally.

'I was offered what had once been a photographic studio right in the middle of Ambleside – so I jumped at it. I took it on a lease and opened The Homes of Football in December 1997.'

It was on the main road, Lake Road, as you went through Ambleside, and there were usually some papier mâché football figures standing outside and a sign announcing The Homes of Football. When I first saw it, I was totally confused. How could Ambleside be in any sense a Home of Football? It looked so arty and smart, as if it should be in Chelsea or Kensington.

'You say Ambleside is not a heartland of football, but all the local pubs are packed when they are showing live football, just as they are elsewhere in the country. We are all football fans now, whether we like it or not. Lake District tourists are not obvious football fans, but they do tend to be people of taste, and they were always intrigued by my gallery. In Oxford Street, we would not stand out, but in Ambleside we always did.'

In 2011, Stuart is due to move to new premises in Manchester, in the Urbis building, alongside the National Museum of Football (which will be moving from Preston), so it sounds like a good match, two homes of football, and there he will continue to display his photographs and sell his football postcards.

So are the cards doing good business? Not spectacularly, but Stuart has kept going all these years, the postcards, which sell at 50p each, being his bread and butter. At present he has 149 different football postcards, which range from World Cup venues to little Cumbrian pitches amidst the fells. He gets them all printed by Abacus in Cumbria, 3,000 at a time, which is not cheap but the quality is excellent.

He still avoids goals and the obvious incidents, going for atmosphere and the offbeat, and rarely photographs star players unless they happen to be in the line-up before a game, when they are being presented or are standing to attention listening to the national anthems.

Amongst his most popular cards is one that shows a helicopter fluttering over a pitch in Ambleside. 'I was on Loughrigg, looking down on the pitch when this helicopter appeared. I don't know whether there was a real mountain rescue going on or just a practice.'

His other popular cards include some Geordie fans displaying their beer bellies, Wigan in the sunset, John Motson in the snow and two England fans walking down the street with their Union Jacks tied round them like skirts.

'They are actually being frogmarched by the police, but trying to look not bothered. They had spent the night on a campsite and had been bitten by mosquitoes and were suffering from sunburn, but were determined to walk proud and tall for England.'

Above: Beckham and Seaman meet Ronaldo, England v. Brazil, 2002.

Below: Greenock Morton fans, crying to get home, 1995. Both by Stuart Clarke.

1990. He also covered the 2010 World Cup in South Africa.

The sort of scenes and atmosphere he captures could not have been done 100 years ago, as the cameras were not up to shooting people and crowds out in the street, while they were moving. The old studio photographs, when players and teams, famous and unknown, posed in controlled conditions often resulted in excellent results, but, of course, they didn't do action or informal situations or try to capture atmosphere.

'I love the fact that my gallery did used to be a photographic studio in the old days. There still are boxes in the attic I haven't properly sorted yet, but I know there are portraits of local football teams and players who came into the studio to have their photographs taken and postcards made.

'I like to think I am carrying on the tradition of producing football postcards – even if in my case I go out to capture football scenes rather than having players come to me.'

And I like to think that people like Stuart Clarke still exist, someone who has come along to put a new slant on an old hobby.

Will postcards ever die out? They are expensive to produce, now that paper and printing and labour costs are so high, and other forms of communication are much cheaper and quicker. But they are neat, simple and good for conveying a quick, understandable message or image, which is why so many commercial and advertising firms currently use them.

When those free glossy, high-quality cards started appearing as give-aways in restaurants and cinemas, I couldn't understand how they did it, as I know how much it costs to print cards. I have house cards – for our London and Lake District homes – with a pretty pic on one side

One of my favourites is a gang of young Sunderland fans all in red shirts, against a barrier, looking up in the air, presumably watching a replay on the big screen. Stuart clearly loves football crowds, both inside and outside the ground, the burger vans, the banners and the flags as well as the action on the pitch.

Stuart has had many photographic books published and has worked with the FA and FIFA, covering all the big games and tournaments in the last 20 years, including every World Cup since

More Stuart Clarke. Above: Sheffield Utd fans in the street, 1997.

Below: Arsenal fans inside Highbury, 2002, demonstrating against racism.

and the address on the other. I get 1,000 at a time printed by Abacus and it used to work out at under 10p each. Now with VAT it comes to about 15p each.

However, this is piddling for any half-decent-sized commercial firm, when you consider how many millions they are probably spending on advertising and marketing. The future, therefore, of postcards looks secure, even if it will be in the hands and under the influence of advertising and marketing.

Postcards with a football element or image will also continue, for as long as football exists – and does anyone honestly think football is presently in danger? That it will pack up, remove the goalposts and go away? Not when all those billions are watching round the world and all that TV money is flooding in.

The pleasures of collecting postcards are much the same as they ever were. They are portable, which is a vital element. The quality of the card, printing, illustrations and artwork are much better than anything provided by newsprint, which means they last longer and in better condition.

I also collect old football newspapers, or any old newspapers and magazines with football content. One of my prized possessions is a run of the *Sporting Chronicle* from the summer of 1888 to the Christmas, covering the first half of the first ever Football League season. Fascinating stuff, as you can see recorded the first hooligans and early crowd troubles, plus the changes in the rules. For the first few weeks, all you got was two points for a win, and nothing else. They then decided to award one point for a draw. I show off these early match reports to all my footer friends – or at least I did. The pages are now like rice paper and crumble every time I turn a page. They are also bulky and hard to file and store.

Postcards, even those which are well over 100 years old, are often in remarkable condition, easy to read, easy to enjoy. All the postcards in this book are from my collection and bought cheaply. Very few are in top condition, because for those you have to pay a premium and I am a cheapskate. I go for content not condition. All the same, they have reproduced pretty well, don't you think? Please say yes.

I keep them in postcard albums, just as the very first postcard collectors did, which I label

All Stuart Clarke's.

Above: Young Sunderland fans, 1996, looking up to the screen for good news.

Middle: Two England fans in Italy, 1990, being marched by the police but determined to look cool and defiant.

Bottom: Wistful boy with a ball, Manchester, 1990.

according to the contents and neatly arrange on shelves. They don't take up a great deal of room. They are easy to take down, flick through, take out of the plastics and examine both sides for prehistoric writings and hieroglyphics, signs and messages and marks I might have missed first time round.

For that is the big thing about football postcards. All football is there, even if sometimes it is hidden away in the background, recording the changes and developments, styles and influences which have occurred inside the beautiful game over these last 120 years – and of course in life generally. I really can stare at them for hours. I feel I am looking at myself when I look at postcards of old crowds, people doing then what I do now. Football postcards reflect football and life. And are well worth reflecting on . . .

LIST OF ILLUSTRATIONS

INDEX